The
FICO HOAX

SECRETS REVEALED

IT'S NOT THE Da Vinci Code
It's your FICO Score Code

$$x = \{q + [q^2 + (r\text{-}p^2)^3]^{1/2}\}^{1/3} + \{q - [q^2 + (r\text{-}p^2)^3]^{1/2}\}^{1/3} + p$$

Where $p = \text{-}b/(3a)$, $q = p^3 + (bc\ 3ad)/(6a^2)$, $r = c/(3a)$

By
William Kirkendale

authorHOUSE®

AuthorHouse™
1663 Liberty Drive
Bloomington, IN 47403
www.authorhouse.com
Phone: 1-800-839-8640

First published by AuthorHouse   2/22/2011

ISBN: 978-1-4520-9228-7 (sc)
ISBN: 978-1-4520-9229-4 (e)

Library of Congress Control Number: 2010916463

Printed in the United States of America

INTRODUCTION

FICO SCORE...FICO FRAUD...FICO HOAX...FICO SCAM

Did you ever think in a million years that one day you would be required to wear a secretly devised morality score on your back ,,, more particularly a FICO SCORE....That's right a score that supposedly tells the whole world what kind of a person you are....Are you a responsible person? Are you a reliable person. Are you a moral person. Do you keeps your word to people.. In short this secretly created score will come to define you for the rest of your life. And what can you do about it? Absolutely NOTHING

I don't think when you were born your parents wanted you to be forever known by your FICO SCORE rather than your name...Well my friends that's the way it is today. You are no longer known for your good name and reputation....You are now known ONLY by your three digit FICO SCORE. 500 is lousy...600 is fair...700 is next to Godliness...and -0- is disgusting and shameful and not worthy of one ounce of respect..

For the last 20 years in America our lives have been taken over, scored and run by a bunch of crooks and frauds named the Fair Isaac Company.. These are the people who stole an ancient 9th Century math formula and used it to create your so-called FICO score...And just what is this FICO score you will now have to wear?

It is nothing more than a profit making voodoo like scheme designed to supposedly evaluate your future behavior in handling your moral, financial, ethical and credit obligations.

What it is in reality, however, is an unconscionable, unscientific and unproven phony morality evaluation fraud done by a bunch of greedy crooks and charlatans who don't care for one minute whether their FICO scores are appropriate, accurate or not…All they care about is making truckloads of money off the sale of these defective scores to the Nation's credit and banking industry….

In the book you will see clearly how and why this has happened to us.

AND JUST WHO ARE ALL THESE FICO SCORE FRAUDS AND CHARLATANS

THEY ARE:

EQUIFAX, EXPERIAN ,TRANS UNION , AND FAIR ISAAC

A FOURSOME OF CHEATS AND SWINDLERS UNPARALLELED IN AMERICAN HISTORY

PREFACE

FICO CREDIT SCORING FRAUD 101

The American credit and Banking Industry's SECRET FICO algorithm credit scoring system is nothing more than an <u>Ancient Muslim Hoax</u>.
A fraudulent scam that has hijacked our economy, destroyed our banking system and crippled our Nation's housing markets.

AND THIS IS HOW THEY DID IT

20 Years ago the Nation's banks and credit grantors began to worship at the altar of an Ancient Muslim mathematician by the name of **MOHAMMED BIN AL-KHWARIZIMI** . In the years that followed They banks entered into a Devil's partnership with a company called **FAIR ISAAC Co.** who by using Khwarizimi's ancient convoluted math formula created what is known today as your FICO score. The profit and greed these Fair Isaac people generated for themselves and their customer banks from this credit scoring hoax over the years has been nothing short of staggering,

Today this Company has a market cap of over a BILLION dollars with customers in 80 countries. A Billion dollars of your money that they have scammed from you through their phony FICO HOAX. They say about this HOAX on their website that they have pioneered the development and application of <u>*critical technologies*</u> (*Voodoo Tarot card Algorithm formulas*

4

invented by ancient Muslims)

These technologies they say further include *predictive analytics (we can predict the future)*, business rules management and optimization. We use these technologies to help businesses improve the precision, consistency and agility of their complex, high-volume decisions. *My translation of all this…We will continue scam you forever with this FICO HOAX as we steal millions of dollars out of your pockets with complete immunity. We have that much power.*

Incidentally if you want to know how arrogant and crass these people are consider this. The words FAIR ISAAC AND FICO were devised as an acronym of the founders of the company Bill *FAIR* and Earl *ISAAC* How sick is that? Almost as sick as their FICO God naming the word Algebra after himself.

BELOW IS THE EXACT AL-KHWARIZIMI FORMULA THEY USE

$x = \{q + [q^2 + (r-p^2)^3]^{1/2}\}^{1/3} + \{q - [q^2 + (r-p^2)^3]^{1/2}\}^{1/3} + p$
Where $p = -b/(3a)$, $q = p^3 + (bc\ 3ad)/(6a^2)$, $r = c/(3a)$

On top of this They also use what is called the "Church-Turing Lambda Machine Thesis to help them arrive at their phony FICO Scores…This thesis is described this way…

"In setting up a complete algorithmic theory, what we do is describe a procedure performable for each set of values of the independent variables which procedure necessarily

5

terminates and in such manner that from the outcome we can read a definite answer, "yes" or "no" to the question......"is the predicate true"?

WHAT THE HELL DID HE JUST SAY???

Now If you're not careful my friends you could lose your job, your home, your car, your insurance, your apartment, and your good name and reputation if you don't understand how this phony algorithm scoring hoax works..... and how it has completely taken over our banking system and our economy and our lives for the last 20 years. What I don't understand is how we let them get away with this scam for so long

In my case as you will see I myself don't have a bad credit score....I have a no FICO score. If I wanted to have a score I was told I would first have to get a credit reference from my milkman and my gardener

This is what I mean when I say this FICO scoring scam is the biggest hoax and fraud in American history...BAR NONE

Besides being a sham and a fraud it is also an evil front for racial, religious, gender, age, financial and cultural discrimination and intolerance. When they get through with you...believe me you won't know what hit you...

My milkman and my gardener??? When they told me that

I couldn't believe it. Here was this prestigious Wells Fargo Bank telling me that they wouldn't give me a loan because I had no credit score.... **BUT....** they would lend me all the money I wanted if only I would get a credit reference from my ***milkman and my gardener*** so I could get myself a FICO score.

I say in this book many times that this FICO scoring fraud is the biggest scam in American history.. If you want proof then just contemplate what I just said for a few minutes. How well do you know your milkman and your gardener? Do you think they would give you a good credit referral if you asked them nicely?

ABSOLUTELY ABSURD & TOTALLY PREPOSTEROUS

A Message from the Author

Why am I at War with These FICO Credit scoring people you ask?…It's simple…It's because I'm mad as hell…..

* That every Bank in America worships at the Feet of this Golden Idol FICO HOAX

* That Because of this Idolatry they have hijacked and destroyed our banking system and crippled our housing markets

* That We Americans have to put up with THIS KIND OF MASSIVE FRAUD that is helping to destroy our economy

* That we have to suffer in a severe economic recession while under the spell of an ancient Muslim credit scoring HOAX

Contents

I. OVERVIEW

WELCOME INTO THE FRAUDULENT WORLD OF THE FICO HOAX

I WILL TEACH YOU HOW THIS FRAUD WORKS AND WHAT YOU CAN DO TO PROTECT YOURSELF FROM THESE FRAUDULENT SCAM ARTISTS

BUT before I do that I want to first tell you how I got involved in this Book in the first place and why I'm so passionate about making sure that what happened to me can never happen to anyone else.

THE ZERO MAN SAGA OF 2010

I am not a disgruntled consumer who is unhappy that his credit score is too low. My credit over the years has been excellent. I am now a screaming angry and outraged 73 year old curmudgeon who is unhappy that his credit score is -0- When this happened to me I knew immediately that America was in big trouble.

What more could go wrong I thought when a person had to get a credit reference from his milkman and his gardener to be able to borrow money from a bank. This FICO scam it seemed to me to had run it's full course and in my view had to be stopped immediately. After all look what it had done to our financial markets over the last 5 years. It practically destroyed them...and our economy along with it. In my view then Voodoo FICO credit scoring had to go and common sense had to move back in.

Anyway on June 8th 2010 I applied to Wells Fargo Bank for a small mortgage loan to buy a nice home as a special property to someday leave to my children to live in. When I applied for this loan I was told a few days later that the bank would not approve my loan because *I had no credit score.* I didn't even need the loan as I could have bought it with cash I had...but now I was being told that after 50 years of excellent credit I HAD NO CREDIT SCORE....

How could that be I wondered. I was a 73 year man who has had excellent credit for over 50 years. What I was told was that the reason I *had no FICO score* was because *I had no debt.* You see a zero FICO score is a sign of a financially responsible person....one who does not borrow money, one who saves and invests regularly and pays cash for things. In other words they don't worship at the great Suzy Orman FICO SCORE ALTAR.

In the last 12 years or so it was true that I had paid off all my debt because I was going to retire and I did not want to burden myself with any debt for my retirement years. During this time when I did buy something I didn't buy it on credit I bought it for cash....which I thought was the prudent thing to do.

At the time of the bank's denial of my loan application we had a knock down drag out tempers flaring all out war of nasty words over this. I accused them in no uncertain terms of discrimination against me because of my age and circumstance in life….. and they told me in no uncertain terms that I could only be approved for my loan if I would go out and get a credit reference from my *milkman and my gardener. This they said would then give me a FICO score*

To say the least this was the final straw so I said to myself that I would not let these people get away with what they were doing to me for one more minute. Their fraud had run it's course with me and had to be stopped

What I didn't know at the time was that their decision about me was not all that unusual in the banking industry today when dealing with older applicants who were debt free and had no recent credit history. The fact that older applicants had many many years of previous good credit history during their lifetime meant nothing to the banking industry these days. If you had no credit history within the last 24 months you were sent to the old people's home for bad credit risks.

What they wanted was what I call "Instant credit score gratification" We don't care if you had a good credit history in the past what have you done for us lately? *We also don't care how much money you make or how much you have in the bank for cash reserves. The ONLY thing we want from you is a FICO score*

In any event I began to look into this matter very closely and what I found out was shocking and very disturbing. I found out that the only reason Wells Fargo did not want to give me a mortgage loan was simply because they could not get a FICO score on me. What they got was a score on me that read ZERO... NADA....NOTHING.... AS IF I WERE DEAD AND NEVER EXISTED.

In other words I completely failed my credit test with a -0- score and according to them they had no record of me ever living on the planet. I was merely a lost entity ready to be put out to pasture for the rest of my life. A deadbeat Grandpa with a Zero FICO Score and a Zero life...A complete failure not to be recognized as ever having been a living human being.

To say that when I found this out I was livid would be a mild understatement. I was more than livid. I was determined with a fire in my belly to right this wrong that was being done to me and expose this evil system that tried to make me into a non entity failure in life. Who the hell were these people I thought. Well I soon found out who they were and what I found out made me sick to my stomach.

It seems we now live in an age where people like the Fair Isaac Company, Equifax, Trans Union, Experian and Credco Core Logic (all the people who gave me a zero credit score) think they can libel and slander and defame you with complete immunity. Well I'm here to tell them they can't.....Because ONLY over my dead body will that happen.. I won't rest until I put them all out of business.

I am now in the process of suing all these people for discrimination, Slander, Libel and defamation of character over what they just did to me plus a dozen other deliberate FCRA and HIPAA law violations depriving me of my right to privacy and due process. I'm also suing them in the court of Public Opinion by writing this book and setting up my FICO fraud websites for the whole world to see.

After 50 years of being a good responsible citizen I was now being classified as a non entity who never even existed on this earth. A man who can now only be spoken for as to his character and good name through his milkman or his gardener. Not in America will I ever allow this to happen to anyone….Move over Rosa Parks I'm moving in on your territory. If something morally obscene is happening then you have a duty to speak up and get rid of it.

The exact definition of "defamation" I looked up is where someone makes a claim against you that is expressly stated (like in my credit report) or implied to be factual *but is not*…In my case all these people made false and libelous claims against me that I had NO credit history when in fact they knew full well that I had a credit history for many years. How do I know this? Well Because two weeks later they proved to me that they were wrong when they did say I had a credit score.

This deliberate hoax of theirs fits the legal definition of Defamation to a T. By *printing something false* about me *that they knew was not true* they embarrassed me and they humiliated me and they defamed me.

I may not have had a recent credit history but I sure as hell had a credit history going back 50 years. To say that I had no credit history therefore was a deliberate lie and act of slander and defamation on their part.... One that I will spend the rest of my life going after them for in court.

These people also deliberately cast aspersions on my character designed to maliciously injure and destroy my good name and reputation...A name and reputation that I had taken great pride in working to establish for over 50 years. *A name that they now said only my milkman or gardener could vouch for.*

Well I am not about to let them get away with this for one second. I will take them all the way to the Supreme Court if I have to to stop all their fraud and abuse against good people in America like me.

As I found out I was not alone in this malicious defamation. There are literally millions of other people in the same boat as I am whose lives and reputations have been completely ruined and destroyed by these slanderous FICO Credit reporting people.

My only problem now is how much do I sue them for. What is a persons reputation and good name worth? I don't really know but in my case I have 8 children and 7 grandchildren who look up to me as a good responsible person and I have a wonderful wife and sister who also look up to me as good responsible person.

I finally settled on a number for my good name and reputation of $100 million dollars...Two million dollars for each of the last 50 years I have worked tirelessly to establish my good name and reputation. In court I know my 50 year record will speak loudly for itself over their phony claims that I had no credit history...

The specific causes of action I intend to pursue in my suit are these:

1. A deliberate violation of my rights under the Fair Credit Reporting Act and the Due Process Clause of the U.S. Constitution

2. A deliberate violation of my right to Medical privacy under HIPAA laws and the California Constitution Right to Privacy laws

3. Deliberate discrimination against me because of my age and circumstance

4. Libel, Slander and defamation of my good name, character and reputation by declaring in writing for all to see that... I was a total non entity (-0-) person who NEVER enjoyed or established any good credit history in his life. In other words I never existed. I was for all intent and purposes a ZERO MAN....

The one thing that stands out in my lawsuit is that when they gave me a -0- credit score *they absolutely knew it was false.* Why? Because only a few weeks later they gave me a score.....and then a few days after that they gave me another -0- score again... And then a few days after that they gave me a score again . And then a few days after that they gave me a -0- score again.

My passion now is to publish this book and sell as many copies as I can to put a big monkey wrench into these frauds and charlatans. Hopefully By doing this I can help others not have to suffer the same fate as I have.... and maybe at the same time I can put these crooks out of business.

As a result if this experience I felt like I was a slave back in the 1800's. Make this guy a non entity and keep him uneducated, poor and in debt. Don't let him enjoy the fruits of his labors or the freedoms of his country. Keep him isolated forever from those privileges using our National FICO HOAX to do so..

HOW DID WE GET INTO THIS FICO MESS?

TV AD HOAX

Can't you just see those disheveled juvenile delinquents jumping all around on TV every night shouting...

"GET YOUR FREE CREDIT SCORE"
REMEMBER FOLKS YOUR CREDIT SCORE IS
ABSOLUTELY FREEEEEEEEEE **HOW MANY**
TIMES DID WE HEAR THAT ON TV EVERY
DAY? 100? 200?...

OR HOW ABOUT WASHED UP ACTOR BEN
STEIN OR PHONY FINANCIAL GERU SUZY
ORMAN SINGING THE PRAISES (FOR BIG BIG
BUCKS) OF THIS PHONY FICO SCORE SCAM?

THE TRAP IS BEING SET FOR YOU....PAY
THESE FICO CROOKS $500 and THEY WILL
SEND YOU ALL THE FREEEEEEEEEE CREDIT
REPORTS AND CREDIT SCORES YOU WANT

So what's going on here you ask? Are we being bamboozled by a bunch of juvenile delinquents, washed up actors, and a phony financial crook on TV trying to sell us phony credit scores or is it worse than that? I only point this out to show you what a terrible mess we've gotten ourselves into. Later on I will show you how the credit reporting business in America has mushroomed into a multi Billion dollar con game that is much more ominous than these TV scams.

At $500 a pop times 50 million adults watching TV everyday... that's a tidy sum of I think $250 Million into the coffers of the Fair Isaac Co. Even if they only scammed half that amount it is still almost $125 Million in ill gotten profits. You will be interested to know that last year the company brought in over $600 Million in gross revenue....which if my figures are correct meant that almost 20-30% of their revenue came off of their TV AD scam. I always wondered how they paid for all those ads. Now I know.

And the fraud in this con game gets much worse. I figure it costs us well over another $100 Million more they raked in from all their other crooked scams they operated against us. I think I could make the case therefore that we are being made fools of and swindled out of hundreds of millions of our hard earned dollars each year by a sleazy bunch of FICO con game artists.

FICO Scores are like drugs. If we don't buy them their evil and destruction will go away and won't hurt us. If we continue, however, to fall prey to these FICO people and buy into all their scams then in the end we will get hurt badly.....And If you think these FICO people can't hurt you wait until your read the rest of this book.

As we all know too well when you wield absolute

power over people then you wind up with an absolute catastrophe on your hands. It is no secret that the FICO people in this country have an iron grip and absolute monopoly on all the credit scoring that is done today. If we haven't learned anything from history I hope we have learned that *absolute* power over people (like the FICO people have over us) corrupts *absolutely.*

The word "absolute" means…*not limited by law and no possible room for change… This my friends is what we have with our Nation's FICO credit scoring system…. not limited by law and completely unchangeable…… no matter how bad or how corrupt it is. That's not my America. The rule of law and Give me liberty or give me death is my America.*

No amount of self serving fluff these people can put out will ever convince me that they aren't out for only one thing….their own greed and profit…

They don't care if their system works well or not.
They don't care if they hurt people or not.
They don't care if they help destroy our economy and way of life or not,.
They don't care if because of them you can't get a job,
They don't care if because of them you lose your home. They don't care if because of them you can't get a mortgage to buy a house for your family or rent an apartment to live in.
They don't care if they cause you to become depressed and despondent over what they did to you.

No my friends they don't care about anything but themselves and their own greed. Nothing else ever crosses their mind.

II. FORWARD

"DEBTORS BONDAGE"

Proverbs 22:7 The Rich will rule over the poor…. and the borrower will be a slave to the lender

This is called…"DEBTORS BONDAGE"…..A must if you are to have a good FICO score. If you don't have a lot of debt you will be sent to the FICO's debtors bondage prison for people with ZERO credit scores.

This Debtors Bondage is the basis of your FICO score… If you have NO DEBT LIKE ME you will have a -0- FICO score…Let's just keep people in America poor and in debt so they can be ruled over and scammed by the greedy banks and their FICO scoring masters.

This is what happened in the days of Slavery. The slave owners (like the FICO people) purposely kept their slaves (like you and me) poor, uneducated and in debt so they could rule over them for their own greed and profit. Today we are the ones being enslaved by these FICO BONDAGE people for THEIR own greed and profit

Over the last few months I discovered much to my dismay that after 50 years of a great credit history and owning dozens of homes, cars and other real estate investments that my FICO credit score was an abysmal ZERO. It seemed that I was now being singled out and confined to a FICO DEBT BONDAGE PRISON for my lack of debt…a lack of debt that I purposely worked hard to achieve so I wouldn't be burdened with it in my retirement years

MY PERSONAL DEBTORS BONDAGE STORY

Let me quote from them as to how they arrived at MY ZERO score.
!
1. In my report dated June 8ᵗʰ 2010 They wrote about me....

EFX Beacon 5.0...Score Not Available...No recently reported account information (DEBT is what they mean)

XPN FICO...Score Not Available due to model exclusion criteria...(And what model may that be I ask? You will see later in how these crooks have over 100 different models to choose from... none of which make any sense at all)

TWC FICO classic 04 ...File Not Scored because of insufficient credit ....ie: **NO DEBT**

2. In my report dated August 21ˢᵗ 2010....

Exp/Fair Isaac Auto Score....Not Available due to model exclusion criteria"....(And what exclusion criteria model might that be may I ask? NO DEBT?)

3. In my report dated August 30th 2010 they wrote about me

EFX Credit Score….600…

(What??? Now they give me a score…. (even if it is a lousy one not representative of my true creditworthiness whatsoever)…. whereas 10 DAYS AGO THEY GAVE ME NO SCORE AT ALL…Score… Not Available

Your new score they say is considered (by them I guess) to be FAIR).. Thank God because 14 days later they changed my score back to ZERO again…And then 14 days after that They changed it to 624...And 14 days after that they changed it back to ZERO again

And why did they do this? Because they say:

1. Payment history…Your history of paying bills on time… (Unfortunately for me and my credit score I HAVE NO BILLS TO PAY ON TIME…I'M DEBT FREE!!!) Sooooooo How do I upgrade paying bills on time of I have no bills to upgrade with??

Score…Fair…Upgrade…Upgrade…

2. Amount of debt Your total amount of outstanding debt. (YOU MUST BE IN DEBT OR NO CREDIT SCORE)

Score …Poor…Up grade…Upgrade

UPGRADE MY DEBT???? What the hell does that mean?

3. Length of credit history…How long you've had credit

Score…Poor…Upgrade…Upgrade

(what do I need 100 years of credit history. 50 years not good enough for them?)

4. Type of credit… The various types of credit accounts you have

Score…Poor…Upgrade…Upgrade
(Let's see. How about I go out and buy a new 50 foot Yacht to upgrade my accounts?)

CAN ALL YOU FOLKS SPELL FICO HOAX…. HERE'S MORE

4. Now in My Report dated September 14th 2010 they wrote about me…(This report incidentally was sold to a bank by a credit report re-seller named CREDO/CORE LOGIC. Defective merchandise sold TO a bunch of crooks BY a bunch of crooks.)

Equifax Beacon…Credit Score…Zero

(what about 14 days ago when you reported it as 624?)… Beacon Not Available…No recently reported account information FRAUD FRAUD FRAUD

Experian…Credit Score Zero…

Risk score not available due to model exclusion criteria… (What model exclusion criteria? NO DEBT??) FRAUD FRAUD FRAUD

Trans Union…Credit score…Zero…

File not recorded because of insufficient credit. (I guess my new Yacht purchase on credit hadn't showed up yet?) FRAUD FRAUD FRAUD

UPDATE BULLETIN!!!!

Today is now September 20th 2010. I was just told by Equifax that NOW I do have a score…BUT THEY CAN'T TELL ME WHAT IT IS??? They have to mail it to me…

When I asked them what would happen if I ran my credit score today with a bank….what score would show up…. they said it depended on the model the bank used. (More on this criminal scam later)

The model according to them that a bank MUST use in my case is a "Risk Score Model" If they don't use this model they say my score will go back to ZERO again.

….If this isn't a three card Monty, Bernie Madoff con game scam then I don't know what is…

UPDATE BULLETIN!!!! #2

Today is now September 28th 2010. I was just told by my bank that they ran my credit report from 3 bureaus and **<u>I STILL DON'T HAVE A CREDIT SCORE....</u>** <u>*(Notwithstanding Equifax telling me I did have one on September 20th)*</u>

If all this isn't enough to convince a jury that these people are the biggest crooks and frauds in America then I don't know what will. By the way my bank got my 9/28 report from the last crook that gave me a credit score...Credco/ Core Logic...you know the credit score re seller who sells defective merchandise to all their bank customers and charges them $15.99 for each defective credit report they stiff them with.

To say that I am livid about these people is a MILD understatement...What my case proves beyond a shadow of a doubt is that these FICO scoring models are the biggest HOAX ever perpetrated on the American people... and I for one will be suing them all over the place to stop their fraud and deceit dead in it's tracks before it can hurt one more person.

What All of this is, of course, is a very clever and fraudulent criminal scheme by the Banks Credit Bureaus and FICO scoring company to use their so-called "Scoring Models" to rape people over the coals and steal all their money... WITH HIGH INTERST RATE LOANS...

The banks we know will use the most lucrative scoring model they can <u>because they know exactly which scoring models throw off the lowest credit score. When your score then comes back lower than it should be the bank turns around and charges you more interest and fees on your loan or credit card...</u>

<u>One more thing they did to me in my recent credit score report of 9/28</u>

There were 3 credit Reporting bureaus that were used... Equifax, Experian and Trans Union.

In the Equifax report they said <u>I had no Credit score</u> because...." <u>I had no qualifying Accounts present" (NO DEBT)</u>. They also said they used the "Beacon 5.0 scoring model" to arrive at my score.

In the Experian report they said I had no credit score because...." <u>the Risk score model was not available due to model exclusion criteria" (you will remember that on 9/14 I was told that the score Equifax was supposedly giving me was based on this "Risk Score model"</u>

And in the Trans Union report they said <u>I had no credit score</u> because...."My file wasn't scored because.... <u>"I had insufficient credit "(NO DEBT)</u>

So here I am now back at square one like most people in America today who have to put up with this disgusting fraud... No Credit...No Score...No Dignity....No Job....No House...No Insurance...No Apartment....No

Nothing because of all these sleazy crooks….I'm 73 and on a nice pension so I can take care of myself with these things

….BUT….

What about all those other people out there in America who are suffering through the worst recession since the great depression….Their Housing market has collapsed, there is 10% unemployment, They have No credit and no 401 k savings left anymore. They lost all their home equity…YES They are getting screwed all over the place….and many can't take care of themselves like I can

And just who caused this terrible recession we're now in?

It was caused in no small part by The Big Wall Street Banks who are still worshiping at the altar of these FICO HOAX crooks….Big Banks, like my infamous milkman bank, Wells Fargo, who along with all the other banks used the FICO scoring system fraud to rip off millions of unsuspecting homeowners when they were handing out high interest rate unaffordable sub prime mortgages to them like they were Halloween candy.

Later on I will tell you a lot more about these phony FICO scoring models and how the public is getting raped by them all the time. With all I know about this fraud I would take a guess that over the course of a year American consumers are getting ripped off and scammed to the *tune of well over $100 Billion dollars. About the same as the Government is getting ripped off by Medicare Fraud each year.*

PLEASE HEAR ME MY FRIENDS

**If they can do this to me they can do this to You
We have been hijacked and held hostage by these crooks for the last 20 years...**

I don't know about you but I'm mad as hell!!!! And I'm not going to take it anymore

MY ZICO SCORE

With all this FICO fraud and evil going on you can see without any glasses on how corrupt and sinister these so-called FICO Credit Scoring system models are. Now it's time to look at the model I just invented to score these folks who like to score me. MY own scoring model that I call My ZICO scoring model (Z=HI) where I place Honesty and Integrity at the top of the list for any of these people to get a good score...If they have no honesty and integrity they get a -0- score

MY
ZICO SCORE IN ACTION

"I'm sorry Mr. Banker , Mr. Car dealer, Mr. Credit card scammer I can't do business with you because you didn't score well on my ZICO score so I'm taking my business elsewhere to someone who is more honest and trustworthy than you are. One of you people even got a 0 score that's how badly I think of you"

What I intend to do in this book is to give you a way to score the people who are scoring you. Namely my own ZICO score on the scorers....In my simple common sense scoring formula I say if you have honesty and integrity you can be assured of a good score. If you are a creep you get a -0- score.

In the case of Fair Isaac and the three major credit

bureaus I give them all a score of MINUS -0- because they are that dishonest and that untrustworthy.

If I were to ever think about placing my faith and trust in them I'm afraid based on my ZEROMAN ZICO SCORE they would not even come close to earning my trust and respect. They would only earn my complete mistrust and disrespect. How would you rate your scorers??

Unfortunately for the American public we are forced to do business with these people who as I have said over and over are nothing but a bunch of frauds and charlatans…. AND, I might add to make matters worse, the only game in town.

Yes, that's right. They have a complete monopoly on the credit scoring business in the United States…..and They are crooks of the highest order who use their monopoly to prey on each and every American citizen every single day for their own insatiable greed and profit.

I believe this book is an absolute necessity for you to have as a complete wake up call and a good tool to have if you are looking for credit anywhere in America today…To buy a house…to buy a car…to get a credit card or any number of a million other things you night need credit for in your daily life

When you apply for credit a credit report is run on you. This report will have in it your FAIR ISAAC FICO

Credit score. What you unfortunately don't know about this FICO score is that it is a complete sham and fraud and is a totally inaccurate worthless piece of junk that doesn't come close to reflecting an accurate picture of your true creditworthiness…. and will prevent you from buying almost anything on credit. Is that FAIR MR. FICO??? MR. ZICO doesn't think so.

The reason you are given this FICO credit score is to supposedly evaluate you as a credit risk. The only problem with that is the people who are determining your score are nothing but a bunch of liars, frauds and cheats…. That only do this so-called "scoring" for one reason…Greed and Profit. The methods they use to arrive at this score of yours they keep shrouded in secrecy so you can never find out how or why they scored you as they did

They call themselves the <u>Fair Isaac Company</u> <u>but there is nothing Fair about them at</u> all…..Over the past 20 years they have scammed everybody and caused untold havoc and misery in people's lives…. and most recently were actively involved in our Nation's financial and housing market collapse. In my view they are 100% responsible for the recent sub- prime mortgage mess and housing crises we are now in.

It is common knowledge that Banks in America worship at the alter of these FICO people which is why the mortgage meltdown and housing crises occurred in 2008. I will show you how this was done later on.

The biggest fraud of all with these people is that their scoring system is a <u>SECRET FORMULA</u> known only to them. You don't know and I don't know and even your Priest or Rabbi doesn't know how your scores are arrived at…. And we will never know.

You have to therefore tell the people who run your credit report that you will not accept their FICO score under any circumstances unless they pass your ZICO score test.

To do this they have to tell you in detail *how your score was arrived at* and offer you up some concrete proof that they are honest and aren't themselves going into bankruptcy or receivership. (ie: Like Washington Mutual, CountryWide Bank, AIG, Lehman Bros., Wachovia, Merrill Lynch etc. etc. If they don't do that then take your business elsewhere <u>and immediately call your lawyer and sue them for slander and defamation of character.</u>

You tell them and your lawyer that you won't accept their phony score because *you know* the score they gave you is a HOAX and you don't understand it one bit…..and when you go to court on your lawsuit you tell them we will see if a jury can understands it.

<u>Below is the Basis of the FICO credit scoring system formulas used by the Fair Isaac Company</u>

<u>In setting up a complete algorithmic (FICO</u>

scoring system) theory, what we do is to describe a procedure, performable for each set of values of the independent variables, which procedure necessarily terminates and in such manner that from the outcome we can read a definite answer, "yes" or "no," to the question, "is the predicate value true?" Plus this one more time

$$x = \{q + [q^2 + (r-p^2)^3]^{1/2}\}^{1/3} + \{q - [q^2 + (r-p^2)^3]^{1/2}\}^{1/3} + p$$
$$p = -b/(3a), \quad q = p^3 + (bc-3ad)/(6a^2), \quad r = c/(3a)$$

If you should get an unfair low FICO score or no score at all like in my case.. Then......

IMMEDIATELY CALL YOUR LAWYER LIKE I DID AND FILE A LAWSUIT AGAINST FAIR ISAAC AND YOUR CREDIT BUREAUS FOR DEFAMATION LIBEL AND SLANDER AGAINST YOU

You will see later in the Fair Credit Reporting Act (FCRA) Chapter information you need to know about your legal right to file this kind of a lawsuit and how to go about it.

Finally To all my readers....I am really sorry...I have to apologize profusely to everyone for being so meek and mild mannered in my writing of this book. The next time I write a book about these crooks I'll tell you how I really feel!!! I promise

III. "GAMING THE SYSTEM"

You Will read later on in the book about how the FICO Fair Isaac Credit Scoring Co. and the three (3) credit reporting bureaus, Equifax, Experian, and Trans Union protect their secret little credit scoring system and crooked scoring formulas with their life. They say the reason they do this is so you and I can't "game" their system..... meaning if we find out how all their secret formulas work we will be able to get great FICO scores for ourselves. **This, of course is Absolute self serving nonsense...**

Well maybe I don't have all their secrets just yet (I'm working on it) BUT I can show you how to game their system BIG TIME to screw up (or should I say SUE UP) their scoring assumptions and fraudulent Algorithm formulas so that their FICO scores become completely worthless and meaningless.....and very costly to them in the end after you sue them

In my case after 50 years of having perfect credit they came up with a phony -0- FICO score that I shoved right back down their throats as being preposterous and totally false and ludicrous.

Now I will be suing them for this and just about everything else you can think of to finally put these criminals out of business.

This Book ,of course, is One Way of doing that!!!

With this book you will see exactly how to completely "game" their system like I did. Knowledge is power with these people .....and with your knowledge their little puppet credit reporting bureaus will fall like dead flies after you get through with them.

Okay let's begin your education on how you can "game" these people in ways they never dreamed possible. The first step is to make you aware of what these FICO scores are all about and where they came from. This you will find in my *first chapter*....**WHAT SECRET FICO SCORING MODELS ARE ALL ABOUT**....**and what you can do to expose those secret models once and for all (SUE SUE SUE)** The ride to getting rid of these people in your lives starts right now. I can assure you it will change your life.

Here's my motto for these crooks..."Take the log out of your own eye boys before you complain about the spec in my eye"

From the first chapter you will move on to learn in *Chapter Two* how dangerous all these FICO score Evils really are. After I open up Pandora's box for you to see what's going on with this hoax the next thing you have to learn about in *chapter three* is their fraudulent and spurious **Algorithm Credit Scoring formulas**. You won't believe your eyes when you see this.

Next you will find out in *__chapter four__* about their unconscionable financial fraud and discrimination against the elderly, women and other minorities. They love to pick on the weak because they are really nothing more than a bunch of financial bullies. The fact is, as you will see, that this FICO scoring system is nothing more than a front for racial, religious, age, gender, financial and cultural discrimination and intolerance

The next thing you need to know in *__chapter five__* is how these people attempt to extort money from you on a regular basis. Believe it or not because they're bullies they once again pick on the weak and infirmed….People who have large medical and hospital bills are their main targets….. especially Medicare patients

And finally you will learn about your rights against all their libel and slander and illegal activity against you in *__chapter six.__* It is here that you will find the ultimate weapon against these people…The laws against libel and slander and defamation….. **The Fair Credit Reporting Act**…. and the recent **HIPAA** laws protecting the privacy of your medical history and medical records. As a good friend of mine recently said to me about these people**…"** **Go Sue the Bastards Bill".**

I followed her Advice and in my upcoming lawsuit against all these folks one of my biggest complaints and main causes of action against them (among many others), is their violation of the HIPAA laws protecting my medical privacy.

In the three credit reports run on me there were over 25 pages and references devoted to my past medical history and medical treatment....ILLEGAL, ILLEGAL, ILLEGAL.... All for one purpose.... To engage in a crude attempt to extort money from me having to do with my disputed and false Medicare fraud charges in the last few years. You will read about these later in the chapter in more detail.

<u>No my friends the American people don't know the half of it with these criminals</u>. They lie and cheat like clock work and think they are big enough to get away with all their crimes. I hope this book will change all that ....and we can get on with our lives in peace and without criminals like these people looking over our shoulder every day to score our morality and behavior with their secret FICO formulas FRAUD.

Lord Acton, the British historian, once said: <u>*"All power tends to corrupt and absolute power corrupts absolutely."*</u> Well with these (UN) Fair Isaac folks and their 3 puppet credit reporting bureaus their absolute power over our lives is beyond comprehension. I hope that with this book and my soon to be, multi-million dollar lawsuit against them we can finally bring a screeching halt to all the pain and misery they cause us each and every day.

To help me bring these people down I have set up two new websites to educate and inform you about what you can do to fight all their fraudulent and deceitful schemes. These sites are:

www.ficofraud.com

www.equifraud.com

As time goes on I will use these two sites to keep you updated on my lawsuit and other matters referring to these criminals. I also invite anyone to join in with me in my Defamation Lawsuit.

NOW as they say in show biz....let's get on with the show...I have a lot more slimy worms in this FICO can to open up and show you.

CHAPTER ONE

THE SECRET
ANCIENT MUSLIM FICO
ALGORITHM SCORING MODELS

ORIGINS OF THE ALGORITHM SCAM

Here he is folks….The massa of all your debt bondage and fraudulent FICO scores

MOHAMMAD BIN MUSA AL-KHAWARIZIMI (770 - 840 C. E.)

Origin of the word ALGORITHM

The word *algorithm* comes from the name of this 9th century <u>Muslim mathematician Abu Abdullah Muhammad ibn Musa Al-Khwarizmi.</u>

<u>The word *algorism* originally referred only to the rules of performing arithmetic using Hindu-Arabic numerals but evolved via European Latin translation of Al-Khwarizmi's name into *algorithm* by the 18th century.</u>

<u>HINDU ARABIC NUMBERS???</u>
<u>YOU MEAN LIKE MY -0- FICO SCORE?</u>

<u>There you have it my friends…This is a your 9th Century Muslim Cleric who invented your FICO scoring system model…You could say he is the Massa of all your current problems and miseries….can't get a job…. losing you home……unable to get a mortgage or credit card…. can't rent an apartment, paying high fees and interest rates…. etc. etc…I could go on and on.</u>

<u>According to this man your FICO credit score one more time is calculated this way….</u>

$$x = \{q + [q^2 + (r-p^2)^3]^{1/2}\}^{1/3} + \{q - [q^2 + (r-p^2)^3]^{1/2}\}^{1/3} + p$$
$$\text{where}$$
$$p = -b/(3a), \ q = p^3 + (bc-3ad)/(6a^2), \ r = c/(3a)$$

I don't know about you…BUT after seeing all the evils and fraud these FICO scores produce I really don't like being called an *UNVIABLE ZERO DEAD BEAT NON ENTITY OLD MAN BAD CREDIT RISK* by a 9th Century Hindu Muslim numbers man…Would You?

AMERICA'S FICO CREDIT SCORING SYSTEM
A CRISES OF CONFIDENCE

So how does a 73 year old man with 50 years of excellent credit be given a -0- FICO credit score on <u>Monday, a</u> 600 FICO credit score on <u>Tuesday, a</u> -0- FICO score on <u>Wednesday</u> and a 624 score on <u>Thursday and back to a -0- score on Friday</u>? How is that possible you ask?

FRAUD… FRAUD…. FRAUD …. AND MORE FRAUD…..

I, of course, asked this question to the crooks at EQUIFAX who published these phony scores for all the world to see . *Their answer…. we don't know… and we don't care.*

What you see here is exactly why I wrote this book. Illegal,

46

fraudulent and preposterous credit scoring schemes used for the sole purpose of generating huge obscene profits for all these credit scoring companies like Fair Isaac (FICO) and their puppet credit bureaus and banks. Customers who use their scores to rape the public every single day of the year.

A bigger crises of confidence in these credit reporting companies and their fraudulent credit scores they put out couldn't be greater…We are in the midst of a very painful recession and housing crises that these people were very prominent in causing.

What is so criminal about this is that what they helped cause could have very easily been avoided. The actual cause of this severe financial crises was one that not one consumer in America knew anything about or how bad this FICO con game was.

What they didn't understand then, and I'm not sure they understand it now, was that our whole economy runs on this "SECRET" formula for granting credit to people. Imagine that…the entire U.S. economy running on a formula created by an ancient Muslim cleric that no one understands, WOW…I'll bet no one knew that!!!

If that's so, and it is, then how in the world can anyone have confidence in a credit scoring system like this one that no one understands? They can't….and because they can't our financial DISASTER will continue for many many more years to come. I guarantee it. That is unless we can get rid of this con game once and for all. We got rid of Charles Ponzi and Bernie Madoff so maybe we can get rid of these people. Our country's future may very well depend on it

If you were given a low score on your class homework assignment that you didn't agree with what would you do? You would probably ask the teacher why you got such a low score. That's a normal reaction…but what if she told you she didn't know how she arrived at your score. And then what would you think if she told you even if she did know how she arrived at your score she wouldn't tell you because it was a secret.

This my friends is the exact scenario of the FICO credit reporting scoring system in America today…It's secret, fraudulent, it's preposterous and it makes no sense to anyone.

In trying to explain this phony system further let's look at what our 9th century Muslim cleric said about his formula

Our Ancient Muslim Cleric friend Mohammed Khawarizmi put it this way. Consider a rectangle in the complex plane. Suppose we have classified each of the four corners as being inside or outside of the Mandelbrot set. For each corner we have the number of iterations it took to classify the corner. For example, suppose *maxit = 100* and we used 5, 12, 100, and 67 iterations to classify the four corners, respectively.

Then the *discrepancy* associated with this rectangle is the difference between the maximum and the minimum iterations counts. In this case it is *100-5 = 95*. The fact that the discrepancy is so high suggests that the rectangle contains significant structure.

Suppose now we have a number of such rectangles. The algorithm always considers the most recent of all rectangles that share the highest current discrepancy. It breaks that rectangle into four sub rectangles.

For each it computes the discrepancy, draws the rectangle with a color corresponding to the average of the four iteration counts, and then puts it on top of the stack of rectangles with the same discrepancy.

Next it takes the top rectangle from the stack with the highest discrepancies and processes that rectangle. If the size of the current rectangle is below a certain limit (which you can set) then every pixel of that rectangle is classified and drawn. To begin with, of course the original rectangle is put on a stack.

In that way the algorithm always refines a rectangle with the highest currently present discrepancy and Rectangles with low, e.g., zero, discrepancies.

The algorithm can store up to 5,000 rectangles. If that limit is reached (which does happen when drawing large pictures) rectangles are classified completely and discarded until enough space becomes available to put new rectangles on the stacks. **WHOA ....WHAT DID HE JUST SAY???**

IS THERE ANYONE READING THIS JIBBERISH WHO UNDERSTANDS IT?? OF COURSE NOT...... WHICH IS WHY I CALL THESE FICO SCORING FORMULAS A HOAX...AND THE BIGGEST FRAUD EVER PERPETRATED ON THE AMERICAN PUBLIC

On The Other Hand

MEET YOUR
ZERO MAN CAPED CRUSADER

As you all know by now I Am the 73 YEAR OLD CURMUDGEON WHO IS AMERICA'S LONE CRUSADER AGAINST THESE PHONY FICO SCORES & CREDIT REPORTING FRAUD SCHEMES
I'm exposing them, I'm suing them and I will spend the rest of the life I have left trying to get rid of them

I CALL MYSELF ZERO MAN BECAUSE I HAVE A "0" CREDIT SCORE. YES YOU REMEMBER….. A ZERO FICO SCORE AFTER LIVING RESPONSIBLY FOR THE PAST 73 YEARS ON THIS GLORIOUS PLANET …AND AFTER HAVING EXCELLENT CREDIT FOR 50 OF THOSE ADULT YEARS OF MY LIFE

BUT HOW DOES THAT HAPPEN? SURELY OVER 50 YEARS YOU MUST HAVE HAD SOME CREDIT? YOU MUST HAVE PURCHASED A HOME FOR YOU AND YOUR CHILDREN. YOU MUST HAVE OWNED A CAR. YOU MUST HAVE HAD A CREDIT CARD. YOU MUST HAVE BEEN ALIVE AND BREATHING.

SO HOW DOES A MAN 73 YEARS OF AGE LIKE YOU WIND UP WITH A "0" FICO CREDIT SCORE? THE ANSWER IS SIMPLE.

MY FICO CREDIT SCORE ALONG WITH YOURS IS A COMPLETE SHAM AND A FRAUD THAT HAS BEEN PERPETRATED ON THE AMERICAN PEOPLE FOR THE LAST 20 YEARS. THE TIME HAS NOW COME TO GET RID OF IT ONCE AND FOR ALL....AND YOU CAN COUNT ON ME LITTLE OLD ZERO MAN TO DO JUST THAT.

Now that you see where I'm coming from you can understand why I wrote this book. I wrote it for you, the American people. The American people who deserve better in their lives than a phony and greedy credit scoring company that over the last few years has practically destroyed our country and our way of life.

If you look at my case there is absolutely no reason or justification for me having a ZERO score. They knew that I was 73 years old. They also knew I was retired. And they knew I had no debt which for many older people over 65 is quite normal. And they knew virtually nothing about my past credit history that they should have known....nor did they care to know anything about it...so how and why did they now invent a zero credit score for me?

The answer to that question, OF COURSE, lies in their secret formulas for determining a credit score. When they have no recent hard data on someone they merely flush them down the toilet and say... No History...No Debt... No score....No existence. If you have no recent credit history for us to plug into our secret formula then bye bye and good luck. Call us when you have some debt and pay off all your fraudulent Medicare bills. As far as your last 50 years of good credit are concerned we could care less.

If they can do this to me with their phony and secret credit scoring formula then just imagine what they are doing to everyone else in America. **Mass fraud**…is what I say they're doing to the rest of us. As I say over and over again these FICO people have constructed…"the biggest fraud ever perpetrated on the American people"…Bernie Madoff would be very proud of these folks

It's one thing to have a person's credit looked at by someone who is lending you money to buy a house or a car. It's quite another thing to have the credit they are looking at being scored and slanted by a bunch of greedy computer executives who know how to scam the world into thinking they are God. This is what these people at FAIR ISAAC do my friends. Its time now that we told them where to go.

If you had a person living in your house who all they did all day long was to degrade you, berate you and slander you, how long would you allow them to live in your house? Not very long I'm sure.

Well this is what these FICO people do to us everyday. They lie, they cheat, they swindle. They use computers to swindle us out of our homes, our jobs, our money and our dignity. They show complete disdain, disregard and disrespect for the truth about us. They cost us Billions of dollars in higher interest rate costs. And in general they are a spreading cancer on our country.

You just have to look at the mess they helped cause in the Mortgage market for the past few years to see how sick they made our economy become. We now need a government feeding tube just to keep us alive.

With these people their truth is not our truth, Their truth is based entirely on greed and profit. Today they are a **ONE BILLION DOLLAR COMPANY** with **40 million shareholders they have to face and answer to on every earnings reporting date. If the profits aren't up to par the stockholders will scream bloody murder and their stock will plummet.**

A recent check of their financial history shows that they have in fact lost over 50% in stock value since 2006.... that will cause a lot of screaming and shoving in the aisles at their Stockholder meetings you can be sure.

Therefore my friends from this we know that the American people are nothing more than cannon fodder for their greed and chicanery . If we get screwed so what. That's the way it works in business. You all saw the movie "WALL STREET". Well if you remember Michael Douglas' classic line you remember him saying...For the lack of a better word "**GREED IS GOOD**".

Well in business this is the sounding cry. Not really a bad thing if your company makes cars or boats, computers or iphones ....but a terrible thing if your company makes phony credit scores that destroy peoples lives and sends our economy into a tailspin. Greed may be good for Wall Street...But it isn't good for main street.

As you read through this book it will become evident to you that we are in a big mess today with regard to our life, liberty and pursuit of happiness. People like these Fair Isaac people would destroy those ideals in a nano second if it meant bringing more profits to their company….and right about now they need a MEGA TON of profits to make up for all their losses they have suffered over the last 4 years.

To suggest for even a minute that these people care about you or your loved ones or your country is absolutely false. They care only about themselves….and that as they say you can *"take all the way to the bank and make a deposit"*

MORE WE ALL NEED TO KNOW

According to the three major credit bureaus in America, Equifax, Trans Union and Experian the formula (called algorithmic Theory) for arriving at your FICO score **MUST BE KEPT A SECRET**…because they say if everyone (you and me) knew the exact way they arrive at a good score we would all **"game"** their system to give us ALL A GOOD SCORE.

ABSOLUTELY PREPOSTEROUS AND HIGHLY INSULTING TO SAY THE LEAST

BEFORE THE FICO HOAX

In the old days before this FICO Fraud Scheme came on

the scene back in the early 90's this is how lenders and others judged your honesty and creditworthiness.

1. You had a job

2. You earned a good income

3. You paid your mortgage, car loans, and credit cards on time.

4. You had a local community banker who knew you and helped you get a loan with his bank.

5. You had some money saved in the bank for a rainy day.

6. You owned a nice house

7. You were a responsible member of your community

If all these things applied to you then you had absolutely no trouble at all getting a mortgage loan, a car loan, or a credit card. You certainly didn't need a FICO score…and as a matter of fact there wasn't any such thing as a FICO score back then. My how things have changed…Now you **_ONLY_** need a Phony FICO score to get credit. Everything else I just described is of no importance whatsoever.

In order to qualify for any of these loans or credit cards today you have put up with the following kind of stupidity

TODAY AFTER THE FICO HOAX:

<u>**As I said all you need is a PHONY and FRAUDULENT FICO score**</u> and your friendly Wall Street Banker will beat a path to your door to lend you all the money you want.

And again….what is this so-called FICO score? Sorry

don't ask me or anyone else in the country because there isn't one person in America who can tell you what a FICO score is…Unless you ask the people who made up this fraud….the People at FAIR ISAAC COMPANY (hence the word FICO).

But even they won't tell you because the company they work for has a complete code of silence and secrecy (Like the Mafia) about these sacred score formulas…sort of like the 100 year old secret of the Coca Cola formula or Colonel Sanders' secret blend of 11 herbs and spices for his chicken. NO ONE ALLOWED IN THIS ROOM…

This is what is so scary and dangerous about these people… ***They are all liars and subscribe to the Hitler big lie theory….The bigger the lie the more people they can get to believe it.*** Sort of like those two juvenile delinquents we see jumping around on television every night shouting… ."Get you free credit score" Just go to **free credit report. com**. Free credit report Who are they kidding?

Or that other washed up has been Ben Stein hitting gophers over the head with a mallet while sitting on a park bench shouting…..You have to go to **free credit score.com. Right away or else you'll wind up like these gophers Who does he think he is…Bill Murray in Caddie Shack?**

If you bought into all these lies it cost you hundreds of dollars in secret fees they charged you for your "free" credit report.

In the annals of American life and history we have never seen anything to rival the arrogance and evil motives of these credit scoring people and their scam FICO credit scoring system. As you read on you will see exactly what I mean.

A LITTLE MORE EDUCATION

On how these crooks keep tract of your morality and character

Linear Regression and your FICO score.... What is linear regression? I didn't know until I started writing this book. Linear regression I found out is a method of organizing data by using a straight line through points on a graph...it is used by stock traders everyday to try and predict the way a stock will move later in the day.

While linear regression is time consuming, it isn't hard. And it isn't as though we don't have some basic FICO equation information already. Here's what we do know, because the FICO company has made this information public

1. The solution (your FICO score) can range from 250 to 900. *(Or in my case 0 to 900)*
2. There are not more than 33 variables (Not true) and we know how much each one deducts from your score. (How do your know that may I ask?)
3. If your credit report is accurate (Which it isn't) you have all the same raw data they use to calculate your FICO score (No we don't)

So why hasn't anyone cracked the formula?

The problem is that even with all the brilliant mathematicians on the planet today no one can seem to figure out how the FICO scoring system actually works. Too many variables… too many scoring models… too many moving parts. (and I might add too much fraud)

No single consumer has the data to do a regression analysis on FICO scores. It would take at least several dozen scores to run any useful regression (and probably a lot more, since any scores you could gather from your friends would not constitute a random sample), and one can only get a FICO score for oneself. In order to do this, you'd have to convince a bunch of other people to share their score and all their credit data with you so that you could run the regression.

It WOULD be a great thing, though, cracking the ridiculous monopoly the FICO credit bureaus have on our scores and our fortunes. Too bad we haven't been able to do it. Maybe after my book comes out we can find someone.

The FICO score also has a sociological factor. That is, it's this magic number that wields enormous influence over our futures. More than that; it's a single number that sums up our merit and evaluates our worth in one of the areas that society prizes most: financial responsibility. Now you can see why in my case I was so disgusted that I only got a fraudulent ZERO score…. and that this was the phony score I had to wear on my back that defamed me and slandered me.

This potent, almost mystical quality, as well as the fact that it's such a powerful, personal reflection on our

value, makes people want to know the EXACT number, to know EXACTLY what the secret FICO formulas "think" of us.

AND JUST IMAGINE WHAT THEY THINK OF ME WITH MY -0- score?? Hey everybody I'm a worthless creep. I don't have a credit score.

SECRET FICO SCORING MODELS

THE CRUX OF THE BIGGEST HOAX EVER PERPETRATED ON THE AMERICAN PEOPLE

(Where have I heard that before?)

99% of American consumers do not know the credit score model that is used by lenders.....AND IT IS THESE MODELS THAT ARE AT THE ROOT OF ALL THEIR FRAUDULENT ACTIVITY

You will remember my problems with these scoring models I told you about earlier. Well here is how that all happened to me. I was scored by three of over 100 different algorithm scoring models each of which used different formulas.

How did they choose which scoring model to use with me? No one knows and no one will ever know. What I do know is that it was probably the bank that selected the model to see if they could scam me for more interest on my loan. This they do to unsuspecting borrowers all the time. GREED…GREED and MORE GREED. Now take a look at this next scenario….

While keeping an eye on your credit report and checking your credit report regularly is a good idea, your credit score alone may not be telling you all you need to know. In fact ***most consumers have no way of knowing which credit score model potential lenders will be using,*** and that can make it difficult to determine the true value of checking their credit scores.

Just consider this – when you check your credit score you are given a numerical score, but that score is not necessarily the one potential lenders will be looking at. Creditors and lenders may use one of hundreds of credit score algorithms, and each of these credit score models uses a different system to determine credit risk.

If you doubt the truth of this scenario just consider my case and the following example. A consumer – let's call her Suzy – goes online to check her credit score with Experian. Suzy is delighted to find that her credit score is a remarkable 900, so she goes ahead and applies for a mortgage on her dream house.

Suzy is in for an unpleasant surprise when her mortgage broker informs her that her credit score is only 690, and that she will be forced to pay a higher interest rate as a result of that lower score.

How could this happen? Actually it is quite simple.

When Suzy checked her credit score she checked the Experian National Risk Model, while her mortgage broker obtained Suzy's credit score using the Experian/ Fair Isaac FICO Risk Model. Each model uses a different method to assess lending risk, and this difference helps to explain the wide disparity in numerical credit scores.

FRAUD, FRAUD, FRAUD...AND MORE FRAUD

The fact that there are literally hundreds of different credit score models, each using their own proprietary algorithms to determine the numerical credit score, means that consumers have to wade through miles and miles of dirty FICO swamp land to try and make sure they don't get screwed too badly.

Just consider this list of some of these most commonly used credit score models and you will begin to see the problem.

The Massive HOAX and FRAUD OF THE FICO SCORING SCAM...SECRET SCORE MODELS

Score Model	Range	In use by	Developed by	Score group
Experian / Fair, Isaac Risk Model	360 - 840	Experian	Fair Isaac	FICO Score
Experian / Fair, Isaac Risk Model V2	300 – 850	Experian	Fair Isaac	FICO Score
Experian/ Fair, Isaac Advanced Risk Score	150 - 950	Experian	Fair Isaac	FICO NextGen Score
Scorex PLUS	300 - 900	Experian	Experian	Proprietary Model
National Risk Model	0 – 1000	Experian	Experian	Proprietary Model
National Equivalency Score	360 - 840	Experian	Experian	Proprietary Model
BEACON 5.0	300 - 850	Equifax	Fair, Isaac	FICO Score
Pinnacle	150 – 950	Equifax	Fair, Isaac	FICO NextGen Score

New Account Model 2.0	150 – 950	Trans Union	Trans Union	Proprietary Model
FICO NextGen '03	150 – 950	Trans Union	Fair, Isaac	FICO NextGen Score
FICO Classic '04	336 – 843	Trans Union	Fair, Isaac	FICO Score
Vantage Score	501 – 990	Equifax / Experian / TransUnion	Equifax / Experian / TransUnion	Vantage

You got all that?

THIS, MY FRIENDS, IS THE CRUX OF THE ENTIRE FICO SCORE HOAX

A dozen different credit scoring models out of hundreds more that no one understands...Secret Scoring models that could cost you your house, your job, your savings, your car, your reputation and your way of life.

In addition to these credit score models there are also hundreds more additional algorithms formulas all designed to screw you over like A Ponzi scheme con man.

When you check your own credit score online you may not always know which model is being used to determine that all important number. In many cases credit bureaus are not completely clear about the exact model they use, and that could leave you in the dark about what number potential lenders will see. Until you know which credit score model was used to determine your credit score you cannot truly know what your lender will see.

That is why you need to know which credit score model your lender will be using before you check your credit score to see how badly you were being screwed.

REMEMBER IN MY CASE I DIDN'T HAVE A <u>LOW</u> FICO SCORE I HAD A <u>NO</u> FICO SCORE....Imagine wearing that number on your back all day long for everyone to see....The fact is this FICO SCORE number will follow you all the rest of the days of your life....and never give you a moments rest or peace with the people who run your life....the Banks and credit companies. Try buying a new car or house if you think I'm kidding. If you are under the magic number of 600 you will never get credit again..... and if you get a zero score like me you'll never even be able to buy a nice funeral for yourself.

What do you think ladies and gentlemen of the jury? Was I was defamed and scammed by these FICO people or not?.... And What may I ask is your FICO score and if you know what it is how was it arrived at? Voodoo, hocus pocus, ancient Muslim algorithm scam...? What's that you don't know? I didn't think so.. No one does..

CHAPTER TWO

OPENING UP FICO'S PANDORA'S BOX

1.. FICO Score Evils and Miseries let out of the bag (BOX)

2. FICO scores could cost you a Job

3. FICO scores could cost you your home

4.. FICO scores could cost you your good name an reputation

OPENING UP
PANDORA'S BOX
of
EVILS AND MISERIES OF THE FICO CREDIT SCORING HOAX
IN AMERICA TODAY

"OUTRAGEOUS AT BEST....CRIMINAL AT WORST"

We all remember the Greek mythology story of the God Zeus and his daughter Pandora. Zeus sent his daughter to earth with a secret box with instructions not to open it. Curiosity, however, got the best of her and she did open it. Unfortunately what she found were all the evils and miseries afflicting mankind flying out of it in one fell swoop

Here now we have a modern day Pandora's box of evils and miseries afflicting mankind and the American people in particular. These evils and miseries are called....

EQUIFAX, TRANSUNION, EXPERIAN, & FAIR ISAAC COMPANY, (KNOWN AS FICO).

The list of their atrocities and destructive effects on American citizens is endless.. Here are just some of them:

These people:

* Invade and Intrude on your personal privacy every single day of the year

* Violate your basic Civil Rights of fairness and due process

* Constantly Subject you to arbitrary and capricious credit scoring methods and models that severely affect your way of life

* Sell your personal information to others for greed and profit

* Tell you that you have free access to your credit report when in fact they charge you a substantial fee to get access.

Use their credit reports on you as an extortion scheme to force you to pay bills that you don't owe or are disputing.

Encourage Medicare fraud and other medical billing fraud by posting all your disputed medical bills on your credit file as derogatory collection accounts.

Act in concert and lock step with banks and credit card companies to purposely find ways to lower your credit score so they can charge you higher interest rates.

They also do this with Insurance Companies so they can charge you higher rates for your insurance coverage.

Make constant glaring errors on your credit report that seriously affects your ability to get credit and in some cases even a job or a home

By making these constant errors and putting in false and misleading information in your credit report your current employment status and future employment could be seriously affected and jeopardized

Take forever to correct their reports and once these errors and mistakes are made on your report they could care less how long it takes them to make your report accurate.

Use innocent inquiries on your part to lower your already phony credit score. Inquiries like department store inquiries, checking out bank interest rates, shopping for a good car or mortgage loan etc.

* Give no mention or credit on your report for past good credit history beyond 24 months. If you have a good credit history past these 24 months you will find it nowhere listed on your credit report...You might find some negative history beyond this point but absolutely no positive history

* On their illegal and reprehensible self invented and self proclaimed and self serving so-called "scoring models" they consistently report different scores in different reports on the same day they were ordered.

* Do not correct mistakes or false information or inaccurate information on your report in a timely manner for your benefit. Instead they make you wait months to even investigate their mistakes and inaccuracies.

* They illegally share your reports with unauthorized companies and people who have no right to see your report.

* They do not put anything in your report about your income or assets and how you intend to pay back the money you borrow

* If you are old and you have no debt they will not give you a credit score...and if you have no score you can't borrow even a cup of sugar from anyone. This then is called <u>"financial discrimination"</u> against the elderly.

* If you have no credit score from these people you are told by the banks to get what they call a "<u>non-traditional</u>" credit score. This is done they tell you by getting a credit reference from your electric company, your gas company, your phone company, your milkman and your gardener.

* If in the past you as an older person had excellent credit throughout your lifetime none of that excellent credit is ever applied or added to your credit report score

* If you want to apply to several banks to get a good interest rate on a mortgage you will be penalized on your credit score.

* If you are a victim of identity theft you will never get your report or score fixed or corrected.

* If you pay off or pay down your credit cards you will be penalized on your credit score

* If you use the credit you have been approved for and given you will be penalized on your credit score

* If you pay off or pay down your mortgage or car loan you will be penalized on your credit score

Author's note: The list of all these evils and miseries against you from these people goes on and on and is virtually endless. I am working on filing a massive "class action" lawsuit against all these folks to expose all these evils and miseries they cause. The time has come to put an end to all these Pandora box evils.

Your FICO Score CAN COST YOU A JOB

Unemployment in the Country today due to the recession is almost 10% If you are one of those 20 Million people who are unemployed how do you feel about a fraudulent FICO scoring company trying to keep you from finding a good job?

Asking job candidates to submit to credit checks is becoming very popular among employers today A recent study showed that thirty-five percent of employers used credit checks as part of the pre-employment screening process

Many people, however, have a ding or two on their credit histories --- a few late payments here, some nasty credit card debt, or some medical bill collections there.

We all know that low credit scores can make it tough to get a car loan or mortgage. But many job seekers are stunned to learn that that their so-called financial missteps can also prevent them from getting a job offer.

Credit checks show very little about a candidate's work experience or management style, so why do hiring managers even bother with them? Because some Employers are sometimes reluctant to hire people with low credit scores. Why? Because in their mind their credit score could signal irresponsibility or over-indebtedness *that could interfere with their ability to do the job. What's ironic about this is that in my case I got a -0- credit score because **I HAD NO DEBT.***

How does that then square with an employer looking down on a person who's credit report says he has too much debt? Not very consistent I would say. But who cares with these people if they tell your prospective employer false and misleading information about you. They could care less.

All the employer cares about is what he sees written on the piece of paper about you he has in front of him. As far as he's concerned what this paper says about you is accurate to the letter…. And if it's inaccurate that's too bad

<u>Know your rights</u>

According to the Fair Credit Reporting Act, an employer must request your permission before looking at your credit report. And, if an employer rejects you for a poor credit rating, the employer must show you the report and tell you how to get a free copy from the consumer reporting company.

<u>It is a known fact that over 50 percent of credit reports have some form of inaccuracies or false statements in them and this could cost you a job….</u>

YOUR FICO Score could COST YOU YOUR HOME

HOW THEY CAUSED THE SUB PRIME MESS & THE HOUSING CRISES

How the secret society of FICO scoring models helped to almost destroy America in 2008....and in the process probably helped to destroy you as well

1. Lenders agree: FICO scores are NOT reliable predictors of defaults

To cause the credit crisis, greedy banks and regulators not only condoned the use of FICO scores, but encouraged banks to use ONLY credit scores instead of common sense underwriting.

If you had a FICO credit score your didn't have to show them you even had a job. What your income was or if you had any assets to get a mortgage loan. In other words if you were breathing and could open your bankers door you got approved for a loan as long as you had a FICO score.

These loans by the way were called "LIAR" LOANS" because the banks didn't require proof of anything you said. IF YOU SAID THE SKY WAS FALLING THEY BELIEVED YOU. They were also called NINA LOANS meaning NO INCOME NO ASSETS required...

2. Fair Isaac dominates the credit scoring industry with

its FICO scores.

I knew that FICO scores were pure BS when they became mandatory for most mortgages in the mid 90s. In 2/08, Business Week published a 4-page article on FICO scores saying:

> *... While Fair Isaac was singing FICO's praises to bankers and ratings agencies, the model was breaking down.*
>
> *According to a Fitch study, the average FICO score of borrowers who stopped making home-loan payments was 589 in 2001, compared with 620 for those who were paying on time—a 31-point difference that pointed to FICO's predictive ability.*
> *...*

BUT The FICO scores CHANGED up to 24 points from day to day with NO changes of credit data!.

I could spend months summarizing the many FICO scoring problems and bugs, documenting injustice after injustice and it wouldn't make the slightest difference to them or anyone else in the Credit scoring industry. WHY? BECAUSE

FICO scores exist for three reasons:
- **To redistribute assets from the poor and working people to the wealthy.**
- **To create the credit crisis and mortgage meltdown**

- To make the BANKS & FAIR ISAAC Co. very very **VERY** rich
- And keep all of us in ***DEBTORS PRISON*** forever

FICO scores were not the only reason for the credit crisis, but they were the major reason. Here in a nutshell is how it happened.

The credit crisis would never have happened if lenders had underwritten mortgage applications with common sense and without FICO scores as they did until the mid 90 when Fair Isaac Co. came along and sold everybody a bill of goods.

Here's how it worked

- **Artificially LOW FICO scores enabled lenders to charge high rates and fees to many millions of people who deserved better.** They were all dumped into what they called 2/28 sub prime loans that completely ripped them off….. 2 years at a high sub prime rate and then after the 2 years were up caused them all to go into foreclosure because they couldn't afford the new reset increased usurious interest rate they charged them on their mortgage

- **Just ask Mr. Mozilo CEO of Countrywide Mortgage Co. how much money he made off this crooked scam of his…BILLIONS!!!! Unfortunately for him he won't be able to spend it because he is now being sued by the SEC for**

fraud (Surprise Surprise) This was the guy incidentally who was the biggest FICO user of them all

- **Artificially HIGH FICO scores on the other hand enabled lenders to ignore many reasons to decline millions of applications that were nothing more than phony "Liar Loans". These Liar Loans were rampant during the housing bubble because Wall Street and the Major Banks were making a killing off of them.**

- **Just ask the now defunct Washington Mutual people how much money they made off of these Liar loans before they went bankrupt because of them. BILLIONS!!!! I can tell you their CEO walked away with about $50 Million in bonuses (Off your Back)**

It is common knowledge everywhere that the credit data utilized to calculate the FICO scores is almost always incorrect and incomplete. The credit bureaus implemented procedures to **MAXIMIZE THE INACCURACY** of the data they report. This they do largely by the use of all their phony credit scoring models

The regulators and legislators KNOW that FICO scores are a 100% fraud but do nothing about it.

The regulators are controlled by the legislators and by the administration. The legislators are too corrupt or

**scared to finally prohibit this credit scoring scam.**

BUT WAIT A MINUTE FOLKS...HERE'S AN UPDATE!!!

(Ed: Note).. Rep.Barney Frank and Sen. Christopher Dodd recently passed what is called the SAFE ACT. Following the dramatic expansion in the United States housing market, default rates on sub prime and adjustable rate mortgages (ARM's) began to rise. Credit tightened and refinancing became more difficult. Home prices fell. The foreclosure epidemic was a contributing factor in the global economic crisis, devastating consumers and forcing banking institutions to cut lending or even close their doors.

The public and Congress, seeking to discover causes for the crisis and create solutions, turned their attention to the mortgage Brokers. Many politicians felt that mortgage loan originators had been lax or even deceptive in qualifying buyers for loans. Congress responded and in July 2008 passed The Secure and Fair Enforcement for Mortgage Licensing Act of 2008 (called the SAFE Mortgage Licensing Act of 2008).

Frankly Mr. Frank and Mr. Dodd you should have been looking more at yourselves than the mortgage brokers. You won't believe why these two seedy politicians pointed their finger at the Mortgage Brokers instead of the FICO people and the Banks. The mortgage brokers only did what they were told to do by the Banks. Run a credit report on their prospective borrowers and pull up their FICO score. After that it was ALL in the Banks hands to do what they wanted with these prospective borrowers. And what they did was give them all a loan with no questions asked except … what was your FICO score?

 __Hardly the mortgage brokers fault Mr. Frank and Mr. Dodd. More like your fault and the bank's fault wouldn't you say. And More like our good old FICO HOAX to me__

We also have to remember that Mr. Frank and Mr. Dodd were not exactly innocent parties themselves to this mortgage crises. They were after all the recipients of favored mortgage loans from their friend Mr. Mozillo the CEO of Countrywide Bank because they were a Senator and a Congressmen making up all the laws and rules for all the banks like Countrywide.

If you score was good (Anyone check Dodd and Frank's scores out for their favored loans) then you didn't need to do anything more to qualify for your loan. No Income verification…No employment check to see if you had a job. No asset verification check to see if you had money put away for a rainy day. No folks all these loans were based ***__ENTIRELY ON YOUR FICO SCORE__***….and as such were aptly called **LIAR LOANS** where everybody including the FICO PEOPLE lied about everything.

If you had a good FICO score then the banks completely shut their eyes to anything else but your FICO score. If you had a good FICO score then as far as they were concerned the sky was the limit. In these cases the Bank's also gave out to these so-called "favored" borrowers (like Frank and Dodd) what they called Adjustable Rate Loans or ARM loans. During the housing bubble these so-called "favored" ARM loans were all the rage. Even Alan Greenspan gave his two thumbs up to these loans. ***Only problem was they all exploded two years later.***

On the other hand If you had a bad FICO score you were not allowed to have one of these special ARM loans. Instead you were dumped into what they called a 2/28 sub prime loan which meant pay us usurious high interest for 2 years and then for the next 28 years we will soak you for even higher interest….which of course you wouldn't be able to pay even if had a job, which many borrowers didn't have after the recession hit.

This my friends is the exact definition of the so-called "sub prime" mess. Greedy banks giving out loans to anyone who could walk through the door for obscene greed and profits. Not the Mortgage brokers fault Mr. Frank and Mr. Dodd…it was your fault because you were all in bed with all these folks all along. Go pass some laws on yourselves next time. We need you like we need a hole in our head.

The sad fact is that our politicians and leaders could care less about how many millions <u>of Americans lost their homes and how many lost their jobs or committed suicide because of this rampant FICO scoring Fraud Hoax. I know Mr. Frank and Mr. Dodd didn't care. They were too busy feeding at the trough of all their Banking friends like Mr. Mozillo of Countrywide.</u>

CHAPTER THREE

THE ALGORITHM BOYS

1. The history of Algorithms

**2. Algorithms used in FICO scoring
models and formulas**

3. The Turing/Church lambda machine

4. The Al-Khwarizmi Algorithm hoax

The History of Algorithms
Used in the FICO scoring system formulas
And
Who were the Forefathers of the secret FICO credit
scoring formulas.

ATTENTION TO ALL MY READERS

**(There will be a Pop quiz on all this in the morning...
THE SAME POP QUIZ YOU WILL GIVE THE
PERSON WHO COMES UP WITH YOUR FICO
SCORE)**

**It's kind of dull reading in parts BUT you need to
know the history of America's biggest hoax to fight it**

The origin of the term comes from the ancients. The concept becomes more precise with the use of variables in mathematics. Algorithm in the sense of what is now used by computers appeared as soon as first mechanical engines were invented.

Origin of the word

The word *algorithm* comes from the name of our old friend the 9th century Persian Muslim mathematician **Abdullah Muhammad bin Musa Al-Khwarizmi.**

The word *algorism* originally referred only to the rules of performing arithmetic using Hindu-Arabic numerals but evolved via European Latin translation of Al-Khwarizmi's name into *algorithm* by the 18th century.

The use of the word evolved to include all definite procedures for solving problems or performing tasks. Algebra, the origin of variables

Algorithms by the ancients

Euclid has created an algorithm that has been given its name. The algo serves to calculate the greatest common divisor, here is it:

- divide the number a by b, the remainder is r
- replace a by b
- replace b by r
- continue until a can't be more divided. In this case, a is the gcd.

(Got all that Folks?)

The algorithm of Archimedes gives an approximation of the Pi number. **Eratosthenese has defined an algorithm for retrieving prime numbers.**

Averroès (1126-1198) was using algorithmic methods for calculations. **Adelard de Bath (12 th) introduces the *algorismus* term, from Al-Khwarizimi**

Symbols, rules, and paradoxes
During the 1800's up to the mid-1900's:

- George Boole (1847) has invented the binary algebra, the basis of computers. Actually he has unified logic and calculation in a common symbolism.

- **<u>Gottlob Frege </u>(1879)** formula language's, that is a *lingua characterica*, a language written with special symbols, "for pure thought", that is free from rhetorical embellishments... constructed from specific symbols that are manipulated according to definite rules.

- **<u>Giuseppe Peano</u> (1888)** It's *The principles of arithmetic, presented by a new method* was the first attempt at an axiomatization of mathematics in a symbolic language.

- **<u>Alfred North Whitehead and Bertrand Russell </u>in their *Principia Mathematica* (1910-1913)** has further simplified and amplified the work of Frege.

- **<u>Kurt Goëdel </u>(1931) <u>cites the paradox of the liar that completely reduces rules of recursion to numbers.</u>**
<u>First formalization</u>

<u>Alan Turing </u>(1931)*<u>The concept of algorithm was formalized in 1936 through Alan Turing's Turing machines and Alonzo Church's lambda calculus,</u>* which in turn formed the foundation of computer science.

<u>Emil Post (1936) </u>described the actions of a "computer" as follows:

"...two concepts are involved: that of a *symbol space* in which the work leading from problem to answer is to be carried out, and a fixed unalterable *set of directions*.

His symbol space would be

"a two way infinite sequence of spaces or boxes... The

problem solver or worker is to move and work in this symbol space, being capable of being in, and operating in but one box at a time.... a box is to admit of but two possible conditions, i.e. being empty or unmarked, and having a single mark in it, say a vertical stroke.

"One box is to be singled out and called the starting point. ...a specific problem is to be given in symbolic form by a finite number of boxes - input - being marked with a stroke. Likewise the answer - output - is to be given in symbolic form by such a configuration of marked boxes....

"A set of directions applicable to a general·problem sets up a deterministic process when applied to each specific problem. This process will terminate only when it comes to the direction of type stop."

Turing and the human computer

Alan Turing's work (1936-1937) preceded that of Stibitz (1937); it is unknown if Stibitz knew of the work of Turing. Turing's biographer believed that Turing's use of a typewriter-like model derived from a youthful interest: he had dreamt of inventing typewriters as a boy; Mrs. Turing had a typewriter and he could well have begun by asking himself what was meant to make a typewriter really mechanical.

Given the prevalence of Morse code and telegraphy, ticker tape machines, and Teletypes we might conjecture that all were influences.

Turing - his model of computation is now called a _Turing machine_ - begins, as did Post, with an analysis of a human computer that he whittles down to a simple set of basic motions and "states of mind". But he continues a step further and creates his machine as a model of computation of numbers :

> _"Computing is normally done by writing certain symbols on paper. We may suppose this paper is divided into squares like a child's arithmetic book... I assume then that the computation is carried out on one-dimensional paper, i.e. on a tape divided into squares. I shall also suppose that the number of symbols which may be printed is finite..."_

"The behavior of the computer at any moment is determined by the symbols which he is observing, and his "state of mind" at that moment. We may suppose that there is a bound B to the number of symbols or squares which the computer can observe at one moment. If he wishes to observe more, he must use successive observations. We will also suppose that the number of states of mind which need be taken into account is finite..."

"Let us imagine that the operations performed by the computer to be split up into 'simple operations' which are so elementary that it is not easy to imagine them further divided".

Turing's reduction yields the following:
> _"The simple operations must therefore include:_

1) Changes of the symbol on one of the observed squares
2) Changes of one of the squares observed to another square within L squares of one of the previously observed squares."

"It may be that some of these changes necessarily invoke a change of state of mind. The most general single operation must therefore be taken to be one of the following:

"1) A possible change (a) of symbol together with a possible change of state of mind.
"2) A possible change (b) of observed squares, together with a possible change of state of mind".
"We may now construct a machine to do the work of this computer."

J. Barkley Rosser (1939) boldly defined an effective mathematical method in the following manner:

"'Effective method' is used here in the rather special sense of a method each step of which is precisely determined and which is certain to produce the answer in a finite number of steps. With this special meaning, three different precise definitions have been given to date.
 (1). The simplest of these to state (due to Post and Turing) says essentially that an effective method of solving certain sets of problems exists if one can build a machine which will then solve any problem of the set with no human intervention beyond inserting the question and (later) reading the answer.

All three definitions are equivalent, so it doesn't matter which one is used. Moreover, the fact that all three are equivalent is a very strong argument for the correctness of any one."

(1) Rosser references the work of Church and Kleene and their definition of i-definability; Herbrand and Gödel and their use of recursion; Post and Turing in their mechanism-models of computation.

The algorithmic theory of Kleene

<u>Stephen C. Kleene (1943)</u> defined his now-famous thesis known as the "Church-Turing Thesis". In this context:

<u>HERE IT IS ONCE AGAIN FOLKS....YOUR FICO SCORING MODEL EXPLAINED</u>

" *Algorithmic theories... In setting up a complete algorithmic theory, what we do is to describe a procedure, performable for each set of values of the independent variables, which procedure necessarily terminates and in such manner that from the outcome we can read a definite answer, "yes" or "no," to the question, "is the predicate value true?"*

<u>PLUS....YOUR ALGORITHMIC FORMULA EQUATION ONE MORE TIME (For Emphasis)</u>

$$x = \{q + [q^2 + (r-p^2)^3]^{1/2}\}^{1/3} + \{q - [q^2 + (r-p^2)^3]^{1/2}\}^{1/3} + p$$

where
$p = -b/(3a)$, $q = p^3 + (bc-3ad)/(6a^2)$, $r = c/(3a)$

WOW DID EVERYBODY GET ALL THAT? I SURE DIDN'T AND I WROTE IT.

I DON'T KNOW ABOUT YOU BUT I DIDN'T UNDERSTAND ONE WORD OF ALL THIS JIBBERISH

POP QUIZ....

HAVE THE PERSON WHO TELLS YOU WHAT YOUR SCORE IS TO DESCRIBE TO YOU IN DETAIL EXACTLY HOW YOUR SCORE WAS CALCULATED AND ARRIVED AT.

If they fail the quiz call your lawyer ASAP and sue them for every penny they have..

CHAPTER FOUR

INVIDIOUS FINANCIAL DISCRIMINATION

(DEBTORS FICO BONDAGE SCORE)

1. *Get as much debt as you can! If you do your FICO score will skyrocket.* On the other hand…If you have no debt your score will plummet and you will be forever discriminated against

2. If your are elderly, a woman or a minority you will wind up with either a very low FICO score or NO score at all.

3. If you have no recent credit history you are merely pit into the trash can like last week's garbage.

4. If you have a ZERO score you can't borrow a dime for a cup of coffee.

- **HERE IS A PETITION I RECENTLY DUG UP AGAINST THE FAIR ISAAC (FICO) CORPORATION**

(Very Interesting)

TO: THE FAIR ISAAC CO.

Stop FICO score discrimination!

- **Target:** Fair Isaac Corp

- Fair Isaac Corp (FICO) determines the criteria for all Americans which can impact their ability to obtain credit at a reasonable rate. Fair Isaac makes assessments on individual character based on criteria which is discriminatory against millions of Americans. I have seen people orphaned without parents or a support system judged by the same criteria as one from a stable affluent family.

- Clearly there is competitive advantage in the American financial system not reflected in such scoring systems and by which millions of people are being character assassinated, defamed, and slandered.

We petition Fair Isaac to come up with a credit scoring model which reflects financial vulnerability with respect to financial actions by the individual. An individual can have excellent credit then have it so easily blown through factors beyond that person's control. Give a voice to those the current credit system stifles!

Higher than normal at risk individuals need a credit scoring adjustment that reflects that handicap or the anomalous credit activity due to unforeseen, uncontrollable factors which put them at substantially higher risk of default through **NO FAULT OF THEIR OWN.**

Your model does not reflect in any accurate way the

challenges i have faced with respect to the normal population. As an individual, I have had to absorb through character assassination sub par economic performance. Hundreds of thousands, if not millions, of other Americans have also.

Fair Isaac Corp (FICO) determines the criteria for all Americans which can impact their ability to obtain credit at a reasonable rate. Fair Isaac makes assessments on individual character based on criteria which is **discriminatory against millions of Americans**. I have seen people orphaned without parents or a support system judged by the same criteria as one from a stable affluent family. Clearly there is competitive advantage in the American financial system not reflected in such scoring systems and by which millions of people are being character assassinated, defamed, and slandered.

We petition Fair Isaac to come up with a credit scoring model which reflects financial vulnerability with respect to financial actions by the individual. An individual can have excellent credit then have it so easily blown through factors beyond that person's control. Give a voice to those the current credit system stifles! Higher than normal at risk individuals need a credit scoring adjustment

FICO does not take into account unforeseeable circumstances or individuals at exceptionally high financial risk through no fault of their own. Orphans, widows, the involuntarily laid off and more are not represented in the model. The model suggests individual irresponsibility whereas these individuals by circumstance are placed into a higher position of financial vulnerability in higher proportion than the average population. Why penalize people already in a downtrodden state?

<u>FICO scoring has caused people to judge other people unfairly based on a number!</u> And that number does not reflect whether someone is able to currently pay for a decent place to live or be a good employee it only reflects past financial difficulties! It prevents many from having a place to live or a good job to enable them to pay any bills or have a better life!

 It is not fair that just because of not being able to pay some past medical bills or a few payments caused by being uninsured or unemployed in the past that someone should be judged years later on whether they are "worthy" of a decent place to live, a reliable car to drive or even a better paying job!

<u>This is America and Americans are being denied the "right" to obtain the "American Dream" due to problems in their past that more than likely were not something done "on purpose" or that they even had any control over!</u>

This needs to change or be stopped before it totally destroys lives, liberties and any pursuit of happiness for so many American citizens that deserve and are worthy of respect and being simply treated fairly!

Doesn't anyone deserve a second chance or have we now

decided it's just okay to condemn people based on what they have done and not on what they are doing or what they can do? How can it possibly be fair or how could there even be ANY reason to deny ANYONE respect or the ability to obtain a decent life for themselves or their family?

It's the present and the future that should be considered not the past! This is just wrong and needs to be made right before more people have to suffer - especially innocent children who are denied a nice home to live in, a decent car to ride in, a family vacation maybe or even parents that are able to provide for them because someone decided to judge unfairly due to something that may have happened even before they were born!

(Ed note: Very Good Thoughts these people offered but no one ever listened. No one except me that is...I will gladly take on the mantle there people laid out which I am doing in this book. I thank them for their words and their passion. Let's hope someone will listen to me

The only thing they got wrong was that The FAIR ISAAC (FICO) COMPANY would never come up with a fairer scoring model because they would lose millions if they couldn't scam people off the phony models they now have.

What the American people don't really understand is that there is nothing FAIR about the FAIR ISAAC Co. at all. These are people who have an absolute monopoly on the credit scoring business and who are a ONE BILLION

DOLLAR COMPANY that operates on a complete lie for their profits. They have no conscience about what they're doing to people. All they care about are profits.

Remember what I said about <u>"absolute"</u> power. When you have it you are not limited by law like the rest of us. You can go on screwing the public for as long as you like and the law can't stop you. That is unless you run into someone like me who is going to expose you for what you are. Law breaking charlatans who will eventually be crucified by me in a court of law...and in the court of public opinion as well.

What can you do about Financial Discrimination?

Yes, you heard me right. ***Financial discrimination***. We used to be worried about people being discriminated against based on race, culture, creed, politics, national origin, or religion. Now of course Americans have rallied for years to prevent these discriminations from being used against people who are trying to get a job or own a home, travel abroad or adopting a child. this is a great thing. <u>Yet somehow the people who do not think everyone is equal under the law always come up with some new form of discrimination to foist upon the unassuming American Public.</u>

As we just saw ***Financial Discrimination*** in the FICO scoring system is pervasive and rampant In a nutshell we now have bankers and credit reporting agencies telling employers, apartment owners, other banks and even private security agencies and independent investigators that certain people are not viable in society ***because they have a low or poor credit score!***

So, if you belong to a small, deeply enculturated community, let's say like the Amish for example. You can be denied loans or a job or a home simply because some reporting agency thinks you are a "bad risk." If you are poor, Black and living on the wrong side of town, you *will* have a serious credit score problem. this can be and will be used against you if you try to get a job or rent and apartment, etc.

If you are middle class and have fallen on hard times with bad credit card debt or a failed mortgage you will find it extremely hard to find a decent job in order to dig yourself out of debt. And finally if you are an elderly retired person with no debt you will have no credit score at all. That's right a ZERO credit score which means you couldn't borrow a cup of sugar from your neighbor.

Of course the reporting agencies and banks and credit card companies want us all to be broke. We are way better earners for them that way; as they can put more and more late fees, hidden fees and rate hikes on us. Being broke we are all cash cows who keep getting milked for small amounts until we are drained. Then the rest of our money goes into the pockets of some bankruptcy attorneys, the IRS and the creditors. Even if the creditors get pennies on the dollar, they know you will be ready for more credit soon after you file for bankruptcy!

The banks are paying off the TARP money to the government and they are getting it all from jacked up fees and credit rate hikes!

KEEP EVERYBODY BROKE AND IN DEBT

In big business the best way to keep people broke and on the edge of financial ruin, is to ruin their ability to get financing or jobs! Hence the Credit Reporting Agencies have taken it upon themselves to become the Over Lord and Masters of our Money...... making sure only those who already have enough, will get more. Without a job or medical insurance you actually become a burden on society. But for the banks and creditors you become a fountain of blood they can drink from like vampires! And when you are gone, you are promptly forgotten.

As it stands right now, if you go to apply for a job or a loan you will not be told why you are being turned down. Although I know of one case of a person who was told flat out that she could not be a cashier at a local grocers (a position she had for three years previously), because her credit score was so low, they were afraid she would steal from them!

So that's what it has come down to here in America? If someone is afraid of you...like they used to be afraid of Japanese Americans during WWII...then they have a right to deny you a job or a loan or a home based on that trumped up fear!? How does that work with human rights again? You're afraid I will steal from you, so you won't allow me to work for a living? Do you think maybe that might force someone to steal when they have no food?

My opinion is this. No one should have the right to view my credit report or make any opinions about it as far as work is concerned. **(Or anything else for that matter when the scores they are handing out are nothing but a massive fraud and hoax)** If there is something on that report that the employer does not like, he should be forced by law to point it out and tell you. You should be able to see any and all reports that dig into your personal and financial background under the Freedom of Information Act.

We need to make employers and others like real estate agencies and apartment building owners, stop looking for "what ifs" and holding all people "Innocent until proven guilty." That is the *RULE OF LAW* everyone is talking about! You simply cannot look cross-eyed at someone and say "I think that person may steal from me," or" He might not pay me my rent," or "She might not pay me my money back..."

Might not, probably won't, and I'm Scared" are *not* reasons for denying people jobs and homes. Especially now in this financial melt down when nearly everyone has a dark stain on their credit report. We've been allowing the banks and credit agencies too much free rein for too long.

Time to rein in their paranoia's and their skeptical attitudes which are nothing more than basic discriminations of rich against poor. **These credit reports are now used as sounding boards for someone's character are** also a front for racial, religious, cultural and other discriminations.

We need action now so that Americans can get back to work and be trusted to pay their way! Let's stop the banks and creditors from draining our life's blood, ruining our economy and destroying *all the classes* but their own

CHAPTER FIVE

CALL ME A DOCTOR FAST.... MY FICO SCORE
IS GETTING SICK

FICO SCORING
&
MEDICAL BILL EXTORTION SCHEMES

1. Disputed and/or fraudulent Medical Collection accounts are listed on your credit report as delinquent

2. Collection agencies threaten you that if you don't pay your bill (or the Insurance Company doesn't pay your bill) then you will be placed on the FICO scoring and credit reporting dead beat delinquent hit list

3. Medical Bills can make your credit sick

4. How this extortion scheme works

Medical Debt Collection FICO Fraud, Medicare Fraud and Attempted Extortion

In summary here's how your Credit Reporting Agencies and FICO score people use extortion methods to try and force you to pay disputed and false medical charges.

A hospital claims you owe them money.

The insurer and you both agree that the hospital's claim is groundless. Despite your explanations of this to the hospital, they insist that you pay.

<u>They threaten to turn you over to a collection agency and damage your credit rating if you don't.</u>

You're not alone in this experience. The exact same thing happened to someone I knew well; I'll call her Mary. Here's Mary's story, and here's how she solved the problem.

Mary owned a health insurance policy whose contract stated, "Sonograms at Hospital X are covered 100%, with no patient co-pay."

Mary went to Hospital X for a sonogram.

Later, Mary got a bill from the hospital charging some amount for the sonogram, but adding a $250 "facilities charge". The insurance paid for everything but that "facilities charge", which they refused to cover.

Despite repeated inquiries, the hospital was never able to explain the "facilities charge", other than to state that it was a standard charge.

The insurance company repeatedly refused to cover it, stating that it was not a standard charge. Even the doctor who performed the sonogram agreed that there should not have been a "facilities charge".

Mary mailed the hospital certified letters disputing the charge, but the hospital claimed never to receive them. She then requested by telephone a written explanation for the charge, which the hospital promised to supply, but never did.

During this dispute, the hospital continued sending Mary scary looking bills marked "PAST DUE". Eventually, a bill arrived marked "FINAL NOTICE", which stated that if Mary didn't make payment within 30 days, her account would be turned over to a collection agency and a delinquency would be noted on her credit report.

So, Mary paid the bill and immediately filed a suit in small claims court against both the hospital and the insurance company, as jointly and severally liable defendants, for the amount of the bill, with the basis of the claim being breach of contract (by the insurer), extortion (by the hospital), and unjust enrichment (by the hospital).

A couple of days before the trial, the hospital's attorney called Mary, apologized profusely for their sloppiness, and issued her a full refund plus court costs in exchange for her dropping the case.

But, I fear Mary's approach may not have been the legally correct approach. I suspect that the hospital could have claimed that by Mary paying the bill, she waived any right to dispute it.

So, getting to your general, theoretical question:

If a creditor, without a valid claim against you, threatens to refer you to debt collection or note a delinquency on your

credit report, do you have any recourse?

YES YOU DO

Section 1681s-2(a)(1)(A) of the FCRA law states:

A person shall not furnish any information relating to a consumer to any consumer reporting agency if the person knows or has reasonable cause to believe that the information is inaccurate.

Section 1681s-2(a)(1)(B) states:

A person shall not furnish information relating to a consumer to any consumer reporting agency if--

(i) the person has been notified by the consumer, at the address specified by the person for such notices, that specific information is inaccurate; and

(ii) the information is, in fact, inaccurate.

If you sue the creditor under this statute, then the matter of whether the creditor has a valid claim against you becomes a matter of fact to be tried by the court. **This gives you your day in court.**

See Nelson v. Chase Manhattan Mortgage Corporation, U.S. Court Of Appeals for the 9th Circuit, No. 00-15946, for an example of an individual using the FCRA to go after a bank that inaccurately reported a bankruptcy on his account with a credit reporting agency.

Unfortunately, by the time you go after the creditor for violating this statute, your credit score rating is probably already damaged.

On the plus side, you have one more party whom you can compel to help fix the problem: The FCRA also puts the credit reporting agency on the hook to ensure that the reported information is accurate.

See Stevenson vs. TRW Inc., U.S. Court of Appeals, 5th Circuit, No. 91-7142, in which an individual successfully used the FCRA to go after a credit reporting agency for not deleting false information from his credit report after he supplied evidence that it was false.

See, also, Cushman v. Trans Union Corporation, U.S. Court of Appeals, 3rd Circuit, 115 F.3d 220, in which an individual successfully sued a credit reporting agency for failing to delete false information from her credit report after she repeatedly noted its falsity.

Medical bills can make your credit sick

When I walked out of the hospital several years ago after having surgery for lung cancer, I assumed the worst was over. Never in a million years did I ever think my nightmare was not really over as far as the cost for my treatment was concerned. My hospital bill alone it turned out was over $100,000 and additional doctor bills were in the neighborhood of $40,000

I never really gave this kind of thing too much thought because being in my 60's I had worked for 40 years and had paid faithfully into my Medicare account to handle such bills as these.

Over the next few years, however, I became disgusted with the medical billing practices of some of these hospitals and physicians that treated me for my cancer. It seemed to me that all many of them were doing was trying to defraud Medicare. Soon I was caught up on a maze of medical bills and charges that I couldn't make heads or tails out of. It was at this point that I literally became a Medicare Cop....making sure that I was being billed properly and that all the charges I was being billed for were legitimate..

Guess what....I discovered that many of the charges were NOT legitimate. At that point I started to refuse to pay those charges I thought were part of a Medicare fraud scheme. (In case there may be some people who don't think Medicare fraud goes on I just recently found out that in the state of Florida it is a $20 BILLION dollar rip off of the Federal Government)

Cases like mine have become increasingly common as more and more consumers find themselves caught in the crossfire between their doctors and their health insurance companies or Medicare coverage. Here's how it happens:

Your hospital or physician submits a bill to your health care organization or insurance company. For whatever reason, payment is delayed or denied entirely. Meanwhile, you quite logically refuse to pay as I did when I thought things were not quite right with the bills I was receiving

What happens next is that your doctor or hospital then turns your bills over to a collection agency. It reports your debt as delinquent to the credit reporting agencies and commences hounding you to pay up. Typically, the doctor's office is not the one reporting to the credit reporting agency, it is the collection agency that is putting all the "negative collection account" dings on your report.

This, of course is about as unfair as it gets because once that blemish appears on your credit report, it's going to stay there for seven years unless you can prove it is not legitimate. Here's another personal example of medical billing fraud I had to deal with in the past.

Several years ago I went into a hospital in Las Vegas for a problem I was having with my Atrial Fibrilation condition. The ER doctor quickly took care of me and I was out of the emergency room in about 15 minutes.

About a month later I got an Explanation of Benefit report from my Insurance company showing that they had paid the hospital over $16,000 in charges for my hospital visit. HELLO…$16,000 for 15 minute hospital ER stay.

Well to make a long story short my Insurance company needless to say refused their claim and demanded their money back and it took me 6 months to get this fraud cleared up. In the meantime I was hounded by the hospital collection agency to pay up or else….and what was the or else? Putting my now so-called $16,000 "delinquent hospital account" on my credit report.

I did finally report these folks to the Nevada State Medical board and the local Las Vegas district Attorney's office. When I did this the matter finally was resolved.

And finally here is one more medical fraud experience my wife had recently. She had a bad headache one day so she went to the doctor who sent her over to get an MRI done. When they told her they needed to do several MRI tests she didn't know what they might be looking for so she agreed to undergo the 3 more tests.

About a month later I got a bill in the mail from the MRI people for over $12,000...Here we go again I thought…Insurance and medical billing fraud just like I had experienced in Las Vegas.

As of the writing of this book this matter still hasn't been resolved but you can be sure that this now so-called "delinquent" account is prominently displayed on my wife's credit report…This despite our fighting this fraud in court and with the California State Attorney General's office.

No my friends this medical collection fraud is rampant in the country today. In my most recent case of lung cancer treatment I have over 25 so-called "delinquent medical account collections" on my credit report despite the fact that I am fully insured by Medicare and all my bills were paid...Most of these are for $50 or $100 which are the extra fees they charged me because Medicare would not pay their extra tacked on exorbitant fraudulent charges.

If you find yourself in the same boat as I was in you need to report your credit reporting agency for violations of the Fair CREDIT Reporting Act (FCRA)

Consumers today find themselves on the losing end of an age-old grudge match between the medical establishment and health insurers, one that has taken a particularly mean-spirited turn due to administrative issues often blamed on the HMO industry.

Doctors, frustrated with the ridiculous claims process and slow payment habits of some insurers, have successfully lobbied for prompt-payment statutes. Many states now require insurers to pay up on clear claims (undisputed claims) within 45 days of receipt or face fines, interest and restitution. In Texas alone, laggards were ordered to pay millions in fines and restitution.

Health insurers tend to simply pay the fines, calling the zero-error expectations of prompt-pay legislation unrealistic. In desperation, some physicians have turned to collection agencies to hound you, not your insurer, for payment.

That practice is deplorable, according to Charles Inlander, president of an Allentown, Pa.-based consumer rights group. "They (doctor bills) shouldn't go into collection. This is a tactic that doctors are using to try to intimidate consumers to push their insurance company," he says. "They should be going after the insurance company and not you, but they know it's easier to go after you because you get scared."

Inlander notes that some unscrupulous doctors have used the labyrinthine health care system to double dip, collecting on the same bill from both the patient and the insurance company.
His advice? Get angry -- then get even.

"I basically advise people to call the doctor office and tell them you're never going to use that doctor again and you're going to report them to the insurance department," he says. "It's a double-whammy. They're doing something that is improper in the first place, and then they're really tarnishing your record.

"Frankly, I think that doctors that do that should be exposed, and then they should be looked into by the state in terms of their license, in terms of shoddy business practices."

Credit health checkup

Even after patients recover, credit ratings may suffer. **Julie McAdory, a credit counseling branch manager in New Orleans, says consumers are often unpleasantly surprised to see unpaid medical bills turn up on their credit report.**

"A lot of times after their insurance company pays, people really don't follow through and they don't keep track of it and don't even know that that medical expense is back there. We see a lot of that," she says. "They may have one medical facility and 10 to 15 entries on there from different accounts that they aren't even aware of."

Once an unpaid bill shows up on your credit report, you have four options: pay it, dispute it, explain it or ignore it. Paying the bill won't erase it from your credit report, but it will be marked paid, a far more positive entry than an unpaid debt.

To dispute it, you're going to have to prove that it is erroneous or fraudulent If you can, the credit reporting service must delete the entry.

If the ding was situational, say the result of nonpayment by your insurer, you have up to 100 words to explain on a consumer statement that the reporting agency will attach to your credit report. Will that explanation make a difference to a prospective creditor or employer?

"Yes," says McAdory. "I have spoken to creditors and lenders in the past several years who say they are taking those things into consideration. They are looking at a person's situation and giving more people a break because of things that have happened to them through no fault of their own."

Experts agree it's a good idea to pull your credit report from all three companies on an annual basis, especially if you have incurred considerable medical expenses. People who haven't checked their reports in a while are "going to be shocked," says Kidwell.

"I was just reviewing a client's credit report with them, it's probably eight pages, and on every page I found, on average, five errors per page," says Kidwell. "Let's admit it, mistakes happen. Garbage in, garbage out."

HIPAA PRIVACY LAW VIOLATIONS

Medical collections, unpaid medical bills, HIPAA law violations by collection agencies

Medical collections have always been treated somewhat differently than other collection categories. Almost everyone I know, and that includes yours truly, gets aggravated when some balance is due after a medical procedure.

I personally know several debtors with unpaid medical bills. One fellow refuses to pay any medical bill in principal. Last time checked, he had 8 medical collections totaling some $1,200, ranging from few $15 co pays to $450 balance for an upper gastric endoscopy. His credit scores were way down, but he didn't care. Not a dollar more to those robbers as he put it. **Medical collection has always been tricky, but with the HIPAA laws, many debtors find a good way to remove bad records from their credit reports.**

There was a time, when unpaid medical bills totaling less

than $400 wouldn't faze even A+ lender. *__It was not a big deal, as long as your credit scores recovered or weren't hurt too much.__* Things changed of course, but back to those 'poor' debt collectors. **The HIPAA or Health Insurance Portability and Accountability Act enacted by the U.S. Congress in 1996 is being used to basically tell collectors where to go.**

The HIPAA Privacy Rule requires a 'business associate' that could be a bill collector or someone from physician office or a hospital, to reasonably limit the disclosed information to the necessary minimum, and keep debtor stuff confidential.

So wording like *no permissible business purpose in divulging protected health information to anyone on an account once there is no longer any payment due* or *please be advised that under Federal Statutes. the Fair Credit Reporting Act, (15 U.S.C. § 1681 et seq) and (your State name)'s Consumer Credit Statutes, you may be held liable for the actions of XYZ collection agency,*

A good protection for debtors against collection agencies because debt collectors know next to nothing about laws and industry restrictions, but do know that violating HIPAA laws will be very costly.

So if you are in situation where unpaid medical bills threaten to ruin your credit, try to convince a debt collection agency that by knowing your diagnosis and treatment, they violated your sacred right on privacy.

CHAPTER SIX

THE FAIR CREDIT REPORTING ACT EXPLAINED (FCRA)

1. Your Rights regarding false and inaccurate credit reports and FICO scores

2. You have a right to protect yourself from libel and slander by FICO scores and false information about you.

3. You have a right to receive free credit reports and credit scores

4. While this is a fairly good law it is 30 years old and needs some serious updating to meet the needs of the 21st Century

• FCRA Rights

A Summary of Your Rights under the Fair Credit Reporting Act

The federal Fair Credit Reporting Act (FCRA) promotes the accuracy, fairness, and privacy of information in the files of consumer reporting agencies. There are many types of consumer reporting agencies, including credit bureaus and specialty agencies (such as agencies that sell information about check writing histories, medical records, and rental history records). Here is a summary of your major rights under the FCRA. **For more information, including information write to: Consumer Response Center, Room 130-A, Federal Trade Commission, 600 Pennsylvania Ave. N.W., Washington, D.C. 20580.**

- **You must be told if information in your file has been used against you.** Anyone who uses a credit report or another type of consumer report to deny your application for credit, insurance, or employment - or to take another adverse action against you - must tell you, and must give you the name, address, and phone number of the agency that provided the information.

- **You have the right to know what is in your file**. You may request and obtain all the information about you in the files of a consumer reporting agency (your "file disclosure"). You will be required to provide proper identification, which may include your Social Security number. In many cases, the disclosure will be free. You are entitled to a free file disclosure if:
- a person has taken adverse action against you because of information in your credit report;
- you are the victim of identify theft and place a fraud alert in your file;
- your file contains inaccurate information as a result of fraud;
- you are on public assistance;

- you are unemployed but expect to apply for employment within 60 days.

All consumers are entitled to one free disclosure every 12 months upon request from each nationwide credit bureau and from nationwide specialty consumer reporting agencies

- **<u>You have the right to ask for a credit score.</u>** <u>Credit scores are numerical summaries of your credit-worthiness based on information from credit bureaus. You may request a credit score from consumer reporting agencies that create scores or distribute scores used in residential real property loans, but you will have to pay for it. In some mortgage transactions, you will receive credit score information for free from the mortgage lender.</u>

- **You have the right to dispute incomplete or inaccurate information.** If you identify information in your file that is incomplete or inaccurate, and report it to the consumer reporting agency, the agency must investigate unless your dispute is frivolous.

- **Consumer reporting agencies must correct or delete inaccurate, incomplete, or unverifiable information.** Inaccurate, incomplete or unverifiable information must be removed or corrected, usually within 30 days. However, a consumer reporting agency may continue to report information it has verified as accurate.

- **Consumer reporting agencies may not report outdated negative information.** In most cases, a consumer reporting agency may not report negative information that is more than seven years old, or bankruptcies that are more than 10 years old.

- **Access to your file is limited.** A consumer reporting agency may provide information about you only to people with a valid need -- usually to consider an application with a creditor, insurer, employer, landlord, or other business. The FCRA specifies those with a valid need for access.

- **You must give your consent for reports to be provided to employers.** A consumer reporting agency may not give out information about you to your employer, or a potential employer, without your written consent given to the employer. Written consent generally is not required in the trucking industry.

- **You may limit "prescreened" offers of credit and insurance you get based on information in your credit report.** Unsolicited "prescreened" offers for credit and insurance must include a toll-free phone number you can call if you choose to remove your name and address from the lists these offers are based on. You may opt-out with the nationwide credit bureaus at 1 888 5OPTOUT (1 888 567 8688).

- **You may seek damages from violators.** If a consumer reporting agency, or, in some cases, a user of consumer reports or a furnisher of information to a consumer reporting agency violates the FCRA, you may be able to sue in state or federal court.

Identity theft victims and active duty military personnel

have additional rights. States may enforce the FCRA, and many states have their own consumer reporting laws. In some cases, you may have more rights under state law. For more information, contact your state or local consumer protection agency or your state Attorney General.

Consumer sues Bank One/First USA for Deliberate Violations of the Fair Credit Reporting Act (FCRA)

After numerous disputes with the credit bureaus, creditors and even complaints with the OCC, Randolph Foster learned that Bank One (First USA) intentionally reported extremely damaging incorrect data to the credit bureaus and accessed his credit files without his permission in violation of the Fair Credit Reporting Act (FCRA.)

Mr. Foster had discharged his debts through a Ch. 7 bankruptcy in 1999, but several creditors failed to update their credit reporting to delete the discharged balances. They also did not report the accounts as discharged, as required by the FCRA. *Fair Isaac FICO credit scores are utilized in over 95% of all credit decisions and the scoring software includes those incorrect balances in the score calculations.*

Bank One reported a fictitious balance for the discharged account, resulting in a dismal 623 FICO credit score. When they finally corrected the balance and status, Bank One re-aged the First USA account. In November 2003, they reported the incorrect Date of Last Activity.

The resulting FICO score was only 664, 5 years after the bankruptcy and despite Mr. Foster's excellent credit history and no new derogatory accounts. The FICO scores rated the account as a default in 3/03 instead of 1999, severely lowering the score.

Christine Baker publishes several credit related web sites including the blog about her own suit and she spent several years researching credit scoring and reporting. She reviewed Mr. Foster's many futile disputes and encouraged him to file suit.

In February 2004 Ms. Baker reviewed a Trans Union credit report with a 726 FICO score only 2 years after the bankruptcy filing. Recently she posted her affidavit in support of damages due to incorrect credit reporting after bankruptcy for use by consumers.

Low FICO scores not only cause credit declines and higher interest rates, but also often result in higher auto and homeowners insurance premiums.

Mr. Foster filed his suit on November 12, 2003 against the credit bureaus Experian, Equifax and Trans Union and several former creditors in Pittsburgh, PA, federal court, case # 03-1729. Mr. Foster is representing himself and he recently settled with all defendants except Bank One.

To date, the Bank One legal team denies any wrong doing and Mr. Foster publishes the events and even court filings at his web blog and at the CreditCourt forum.

Bank One submitted several motions to compel binding arbitration. Most contracts require disputes to be resolved through arbitration not only because arbitration is more complicated and more expensive than filing a law suit, but it is SECRET. While there is nothing wrong with mediation and trying to resolve disputes outside court, the binding arbitration clause effectively deprives consumers of their right to a public trial and a jury of their peers.

Bank One had acquired one of the accounts after it was closed and Judge Schwab apparently agreed that the arbitration clause was not enforceable as Mr. Foster had not used this account since Bank One owned it. He ordered on March 18, 2004 that the FCRA violations pertaining to the other account are to be arbitrated. Mr. Foster now has to attend to two simultaneous proceedings in court and in arbitration.

Most likely, Bank One already spent more on legal fees for their many motions and Mr. Foster's deposition than the $25,000 he demanded to settle the case. Money is apparently not the issue for Bank One. They are determined to defend their perceived right to report INCORRECT and INCOMPLETE data to the credit bureaus.

To date, Bank One has denied any wrong doing and reports discharged accounts as charge-offs and often with balances as a matter of policy.

Is Bank One retaliating against consumers who discharged their debts? Or are they part of the organized effort by the credit bureaus, Fair Isaac and Capital One Bank to artificially lower the credit scores of a large percentage of Americans through incomplete and incorrect credit reporting? BINGO!!!

Here's another one for the books…

Woman wins multimillion-dollar Lawsuit against Equifax for Fraudulent credit reporting

A North Florida woman, Ms. Angela P. William won a monumental lawsuit judgment last year against the credit reporting company Equifax. In her suit Ms. Williams argued that she got nothing but a runaround from Equifax as she tried for more than a decade to clear up identity fraud that ruined her credit score.

A jury awarded Williams a multimillion-dollar verdict against Equifax for years of failing to correct dramatic errors in her credit report that led to her credit score being trashed. According to the judgment Atlanta-based Equifax must pay Ms. Williams $219,000 in actual damages and $2.7 million in punitive damages for negligent violation of federal credit-reporting laws. (The Fair Credit Reporting Act FCRA)

It is the largest punitive-damages award ever against Equifax. I myself sued Equifax many years ago and negotiated a private out of court settlement with them.

Ms. Williams told the media that it wasn't so much about the money, but about the punishment for Equifax. I know I'm not the only one she said that has gone through this people need to know their rights. They have to check their credit report and try to be in charge of their credit history. The verdict was a big vote of confidence for people who wrestle with a flawed credit-reporting system and take on big corporations that refuse to acknowledge mistakes.

On this particular case Ms. Williams fought this battle for many years, and, despite all the evidence, Equifax denied almost until the end that there were any mistakes in her credit file. They did the same thing to me in my lawsuit. At the trial, her lawyers showed the jury how Equifax repeatedly confused Williams with someone who had a similar name but whose credit file was rife with bad debt. ***Thus giving her a terrible credit score***

Ms. Williams said she disputed and debunked the errors numerous times but Equifax kept passing along the false information, ruining her credit. After eight years of trying to resolve the issue, she finally sued the company for irresponsible credit reporting and violations of her rights under the Fair Credit Reporting Act (FCRA)

Having had my own dealings with Equifax (I now have a website exposing all their fraudulent practices (www. equifraud.com). It was only a few months ago that I caught

Equifax red handed handing out false and misleading credit scores on their so-called "Beacon" credit report scoring model. What they were doing was giving me a **zero FICO score** one day and a much different credit **score of 567** the next day. When I asked them how they could do this they just dismissed me and declined to answer just as they did in Ms. Williams' case. No I'm afraid that as far as Equifax is concerned they are not accountable to anyone.

Just like Ms. Williams I am now looking into suing Equifax myself again.....basically for many of the same causes of action Ms. Williams based her lawsuit on.

I know that by now you are probably tired of hearing from me that all these credit reporting agencies and the Fair Isaac credit scoring system they use ....**Are in fact the biggest hoax and fraud ever perpetrated on the American public.**

Sorry folks but that is what it is and you need to know all about it so you can protect yourself from the same kinds of fraud and deceit that Ms. Williams and I went through with these people. That is why I wrote this book. I hope you liked it and found it helpful and informative. The philosopher Edmund Burke once wrote..."_The only way for evil to triumph is for good men to do nothing to stop it._

I spotted evil and with this book I tried to stop it

A LITTLE PEEK AT MY PROPOSED LAWSUIT AGAINST THESE CROOKS

William Kirkendale
vs.
Equifax, Trans Union, Experian, Core Logic, Fair Isaac

Causes of Action

1. Deliberate Fraud and violation of the FCRA

2. Financial Discrimination against the elderly

3. Libel, Slander and Defamation

4. Violation of the HIPAA Laws protecting medical privacy

5. Invasion of personal Privacy

6. Violation of California Right To Privacy laws......Violation of CALIFORNIA CONSTITUTION ARTICLE 1 DECLARATION OF RIGHTS SECTION 1.

"All people are by nature free and independent and have inalienable rights. Among these are enjoying and defending life and liberty, acquiring, possessing, and protecting property, and pursuing and obtaining safety, happiness, and privacy".

ABOUT THE AUTHOR

The author, William Kirkendale, is a highly respected and successful California Banking and Insurance executive who has spent the last 50 years working with people helping them with their personal finances.

At the present time he is retired and trying to reform our California Family Court system. He is the founder and president of The Family Court reform Council of America (FCRC) and the author of a recent book entitled *"America's Family Courts...A Cancer on the Nation".*

He is also a strong advocate for children and children's rights and because of his own personal experience with Parental Alienation Syndrome (PAS) he has become an extremely knowledgeable source and help for millions of other victimized parents and children around the world who have had to deal with this problem.

Mr. Kirkendale is the father of 8 wonderful children and 6 young grandchildren. In addition to raising his own family Mr. Kirkendale worked for over 20 years with handicapped children and adults through his association with the world famous Human Resources Center and the Human Resources School for handicapped children in Albertson New York.

He served on both of their Boards of Directors and was also one of the founders and past Presidents of one of

New York State's most successful Easter Seal Society chapters.

Because of Mr. Kirkendale's many years of work with these organizations he was awarded the Human Resources Center's highest honor, the Presidents award, for his outstanding dedication and service to the Nation's handicapped. Mr. Kirkendale currently lives in Southern California.

 Mr. Kirkendale has now found a new cause he wants to work on and expose. Over the last few years our country has been in the throws of a severe recession and a collapsing financial and housing market crises.

One of the contributing factors to this problem he feels is the corruption and greed of the banking system.... and some of the people who support the banking system. One of those support companies is a company called FAIR ISAAC CO..... Inventors of the FICO score.

This is the company who for the last 20 years has compiled a huge data base on every living American for the sole purpose of snooping on them and then attempting to score every square inch their morality, honesty, integrity, and financial credibility with their phony FICO scores

The only problem with this is it doesn't work and the scoring methods being used are fraudulent, illegal and highly guarded secrets causing millions of Americans to lose their jobs, their homes, their credit and their lives in some cases.

To highlight this problem he has just written another book entitled… **THE FICO HOAX….SECRETS REVEALED …..a War against what he calls….**"*The Greatest Fraud ever perpetrated on the American Public*". *He has done this to once and for all get rid of this FICO hoax completely*

For America's sake let's hope he is successful.